CLAY TARGET GAMES

EDWARD C. MIGDALSKI

CLAY TARGET GAMES

WINCHESTER PRESS

Copyright ©1978 by Edward C. Migdalski
All rights reserved
Library of Congress Cataloging in Publication Data
Migdalski, Edward C.
The complete book of clay target games.
Includes index.
1. Trap-shooting.   2. Targets (Shooting)   3. Shot-
guns.   I. Title.
GV1181.M47   799.3'13   78-19055
ISBN 0-87691-275-7
ISBN 0-87691-277-3 pbk.
9 8 7 6 5 4 3 2 1

Published by Winchester Press
205 East 42nd Street
New York, N.Y. 10017

WINCHESTER is a Trademark of Olin Corporation used by Winchester Press,
Inc. under authority and control of the Trademark Proprietor

Printed in the United States of America

Design by Joseph P. Ascherl

To Charles Gage, retired Treasurer of Yale University—a valued friend and gentleman sportsman who, with former Athletic Director DeLaney Kiphuth, recognized the importance of initiating an Outdoor Education and Recreation Department that included trap and skeet shooting at Yale.

Acknowledgments

This book would not have been started nor have reached fruition without the interest and assistance given to me over the years by close friends who have been involved with guns and shooting sports all of their adult lives. To them I wish to express my gratitude and deep appreciation. I take great pride in saying that these men have accepted me as a friend. And the most sincere compliment I can pay them is to state that without exception they are fine sportsmen and true gentlemen: Duncan Barnes, Jim Dee, John Falk, Kip Farrington, Jr., Robert Goss, Harold Herrick, Jr., Howard Johnson, Ned Lilly, Ralph Morrill, Tom Prior, Arnold Rohlfing, Larry Sheerin, William Talley, and Harry Townsend.

I especially thank my son Tom for his assistance in the Kinesiology section; Brad Simmons for contributing his thoughts on "Making the Olympic Team"; Barry Wilson and John Whitehead for Intercollegiate material; Dave Kiphuth for some of the line drawings; Doug Painter for use of NSSF illustrations; and Larry Sheerin, with whom I have enjoyed gunning in various parts of the world and who encouraged me to visit the National Gun Club in San Antonio, Texas, when he was one of the directors of the project during the course of its construction.

I would be most remiss in not expressing my gratitude to Jerry Nicholson, Henry Alcus, and Jimmie Hanemann, renowned trap and skeet shooters, who show me the greatest hospitality whenever I visit New Orleans for shooting.

And finally I wish to note in particular that Jim Dee, for many years one of Winchester-Westerns sports shooting representatives, has cooperated with me in helping to return Yale University to the former prominence it held as leader in the intercollegiate world of shooting in the early 1900's.

Contents

APPENDIX

Preface

Personally, as a trap and skeet shooter, I do not have time to participate in tournaments or match contests. My only experience in serious competition occurred as a member of a U.S. Air Force team while I was based temporarily in Georgia during World War II. And except for a weekly round or two of recreational shooting, all my efforts as Yale University's trap and skeet coach for the past twenty years have been directed toward advising, instructing, and coaching.

During these years I have faced just about every imaginable type of problem associated with clay target shooting—from the very basics of initiating and supervising the construction of the Oliver F. Winchester Shooting Fields at Yale's Outdoor Education Center to instructing individuals and coaching the Yale skeet team for National Intercollegiate Championship competition.

Because Yale's extensive shooting programs are well known, many requests for assistance find their way to my office. They come from a wide variety of sources. For example, fathers who are shotgunners seem, almost without exception, to want to teach their sons to shoot. From their inquiries regarding the use of Yale's shooting facilities, it quickly becomes apparent that nearly all of them would go about the task in the wrong way. Children, and young teenagers especially, need to be guided by specific teaching techniques. In these formative years the youngsters are easily influenced. A proud father, who may be a good hunter or a clay target shooter, may, in his enthusiasm, do irreparable damage by improper teaching. The result usually is a gun-shy boy or girl, a condition as final as that of a gun-shy dog.

One day, for example, a divorced parent, a member of the Yale staff who shares his son on alternate weekends with his former wife, came to me with a problem. He wanted to develop a closer relationship with his son, and since the boy was especially interested in guns, the father thought that shooting would be a natural point of contact between them. The gentleman was an upland hunter who wanted to borrow a hand trap and have the boy shoot at flying targets (the worst possible way to teach a neophyte) at the Yale trap and skeet fields. Because I have a teenage son who has learned to shoot extremely well from a duck blind, my sympathies went out to the visitor. I decided to give him whatever help I could. In this case, instructing the boy myself would not have achieved the desired objective. I therefore set up a system of teaching, through father to son step by step, a week at a time. I taught the father on weekends when the boy was not present, and in turn he gave the same lesson to his son during their next weekend together. The boy's admiration for his father grew, and the father was ecstatic in his thanks to me.

Others who often contact me are the "do it yourself" types, who, characteristically, wish to acquire all the information they can by asking questions and seeking literature to read before they join a trap and skeet club. Although I am always pleased to help, it is a time-consuming practice in a busy office.

In the past several years a tremendous increase in high school and collegiate trap and skeet shooting has taken place nationally. The majority of these scholastic shooters have as their advisor a member of the school faculty who has limited time to spare for extra-curricular activities, or they are instructed by a member of the local fish and game club who unselfishly gives his time to help the school's program. Unfortunately, almost without exception, such volunteer coaches take the students immediately onto the field to shoot rather than following a progressive plan of instruction, so important in the development of new shooters.

With the collegiate world of clay target shooting accelerating at a surprisingly fast pace (as indicated by the number of schools participating in the National Intercollegiate Championships) I also find myself being approached by directors and supervisors of college recreational and club sports programs, who come seeking advice about how to administer a shotgun program. Since the abilities of young men and women students who participate in recreational and competitive intercollegiate programs differ widely, the instructor or coach must be capable of recognizing and dealing intelligently with many variables. At Yale, where shooting instruction is offered to the entire university community, including staff and faculty children, the instructor may be teaching gun safety to a twelve year old and next coaching a prima donna aspiring to make the varsity team.

Aside from personally contacting a coach like myself, it is not easy for those and other interested parties to collect information concerning clay target shooting. For example, to become acquainted with the physical plant—that is, with field layouts, target throwing machines and the structures that house them—one has to dig through numerous folders, pamphlets and booklets. Where do you look for answers to such simple questions as "How fast does the skeet target fly?" "What is it made of?" "How much does it weigh?"

I have often searched the literature for a book that covers all aspects of clay target shooting, a book that I could recommend to beginners, to coaches, to administrators, to my teams, to veteran shooters, and especially a book that contains information on all the shotgun games—in other words, a complete guide between two covers. I found a half dozen or more excellent books, published in recent years by expert tournament shooters, and many magazine articles dealing with the subject of improving one's trap and skeet shooting. To my knowledge however, a single, complete text involved with clay target games has never been published. Consequently, I decided to write this book. And I hope that, even in a small way, the result is a contribution to the claybird sports, because shooting has added so much enjoyment to my life and will, I hope, do the same for my children, Tom and Nancy.

PART I
THE CLAY TARGET GAMES

1 - The Standard Games

WHAT IS TRAPSHOOTING?

Modern-day trapshooting is a game or sport in which moving targets are shot with shotguns. The target resembles an inverted saucer about an inch deep, slightly more than four inches in diameter and less than a quarter inch thick. The target is brittle and will break when hit by one or more pellets bursting from the shotshell. The target is thrown by a machine called a trap, hence the name "trapshooting."

Trapshooting is a highly popular national and international sport. A shooter may be interested in it purely for recreation, or may compete in organized shoots ranging in pressure and intensity from home club events to the world's greatest single sports contest—the Grand American Trap Tournament held annually in Vandalia, Ohio, in which as many as 5,000 shooters may participate.

The standard trap games are: American Trap, Trap Doubles, Handicap Trap, International Trap, and Modified Clay Pigeon. The governing board for the first three is the American Trap Association (ATA). In the United States the National Rifle Association is the guiding organization for the latter two games. Olympic or International Trap shooting is controlled by the Union Internationale de Tir (UIT), with headquarters in Wiesbaden, Webergasse 7, West Germany. In the United States the Union is referred to as the International Shooting Union (ISU).

TRAPSHOOTING HISTORY

We assume that trap shooting as a sport was invented by the British because first mention of such activity, according to present-day knowledge, appeared in 1793 in an English publication *Sporting Magazine*. Although clay target shooting is a major sport throughout Europe, no records have so far been found that precede the 1793 article.

In the days of early English shooting, live pigeons, rather than targets were used. The birds were placed in shallow holes in the ground and covered ("trapped") with old hats attached to lines. At a signal given by the gunner the line was jerked and the pigeon took off in flight. Apparently, this type

Trap shooting originated in England. Live pigeons were "trapped" under hats. When the gunner called "pull" the cord was pulled, thereby knocking over a hat and liberating the bird to make an elusive target.

of pigeon-hole shooting was in vogue before 1793 because the article that appeared in 1793 in *Sporting Magazine* describes a more organized type of "box shoot" where shallow boxes, about a foot high and eight to ten inches wide were placed in holes in the ground located twenty-one yards from the foot mark of the gunner. This box had a sliding lid with a line attached. The line was pulled upon command, thereby releasing the pigeon. The gunner was not allowed to place the gun to shoulder until the bird was in flight. If the bird fell beyond one hundred yards of the box it was considered a lost bird. Wild and domestic pigeons, sparrows, quail and other birds were tried as targets, but the larger pigeons were preferred. Pigeon shooting quickly caught the interest of British sportsmen, and soon the activity developed into one of Britain's most popular sports. Clubs were formed and various types of competitions were evolved.

Interest in trapshooting in the United States started some time early in the nineteenth century. The first formal trapshoot, at least the first recorded, took place in Cincinnati, Ohio in 1831. Live targets were also used in early American trapshooting. The passenger pigeon, extremely abundant at the time, was a choice target, but English sparrows were also used. As in England, the sport quickly spread. In 1840, the Long Island, New York Gun Club was created and the New York Sportsmen's Club added trapshooting to its program.

Ten years later live pigeon shooting was at its peak in America, but non-hunters began grumbling; they abhorred the shooting of live birds for sport. One state after another introduced legislation to outlaw the competitions.

Also, live pigeons in the wild were more difficult to obtain. And live birds didn't fly consistently, thereby, presenting unexpected advantages and disadvantages to shooters in serious, money-prize competitions. Combined, these factors stimulated an interest in developing a method of putting non-live targets into flight.

Charles Portlock of Boston was one of the key figures involved in influencing the movement away from live-bird shooting in America. In 1866, he improved on a "sling device" used in England. This English contraption, which threw glass balls from a trap, had major flaws. Neither the in-flight patterns of the balls nor the hardness of glass were consistent. Some targets were so hard that a direct shot at close range did not break them. All sorts of modifications to the glass ball were made by other designers. In some, feathers were glued to the outside of the target to imitate a live bird, and in others the feathers were inserted into the inside of the glass target. The feathers burst out when the ball was broken. Some inventors added powder to the balls, which, when hit, sent up a puff of smoke or a flash.

Another name, now familiar in the history of trapshooting literature, is Captain Adam Bogardus, who first made his fame as a market hunter and exhibition shooter. In 1876 he stimulated interest in glass-ball shooting by his exhibitions and also by developing a better trap that threw the target in a consistent flight path. In the next few years inventors tried numerous methods of throwing targets from traps, but the most significant turning point in trapshooting occurred in 1880 when George Ligowsky of Cincinnati perfected a flat-disc clay target. In spite of some drawbacks, such as targets being too hard or too soft, the clay targets won instant approval from the trapshooting fraternity in England as well as in America. Ligowsky's successful demonstration of his new target in an exhibition shoot at the end of the New York State Championship live-bird trapshoot at Coney Island in 1880 contributed greatly to the demise of live-bird shooting.

A year after inventing the clay target, Ligowsky produced an improved trap for throwing his clay birds; he thereby established the first real consistent trap and target operation. Many experimenters imitated Ligowsky's creations, and different forms of discs and traps were marketed. But an Englishman named McCaskey put the final touches to the Ligowsky target, creating what became, in essence, the target of today. Ligowsky's targets, made of finely ground clay mixed with water and then baked, were very hard and often did not break when hit. Instead of clay, McCaskey used river silt held together by pitch. Later limestone replaced the river silt, and so the target remains today, limestone and pitch. And although present-day targets have no clay in their composition, being composed of ground limestone with petroleum pitch as a binder, Ligowsky's name "clay target" has remained.

When standard targets and reliable throwing machines finally arrived, the sport of trapshooting accelerated in the 1890's at an astounding rate. Equalized conditions encouraged the development and formalization of the game, with rules that would rate a shooter's ability, regardless of where the action took place.

The first game in shooting clay targets involved five traps set in a straight line. One person was on deck, positioned opposite the center trap, and was allowed five shots. The shooter did not know which target was being released, nor the angles at which the targets would fly.

Eventually, a series of changes were tried in an attempt to make the competition more difficult. For example, there might be five shooters in a squad, one person behind each trap. In the "walk-around system," the squad consisted of six shooters, the sixth person being located behind shooter number one. When the first five had fired, the shooter at Station 5 moved into the extra position at the first station. Under this system one shot was fired by each person at each station.

About 1885, an effort was made to reduce the number of traps. W.G. Sargent of Joplin, Missouri, conceived the "Sargent System," using three traps instead of five. The traps, four feet apart, heaved the targets at angles unknown to the shooter. Within a year or two, the game was being played with one trap, five stations, and a squad of five shooters. And that has been the dominant trap game ever since.

AMERICAN TRAP

The term "American trap" is usually used by way of contrast with International or Olympic-type trapshooting; otherwise, it is simply referred to as "trap." The fact that the clay target throwing machine is also called a trap may confuse the new shooter, for the machine that propels skeet targets is known as a skeet trap and the type that throws trap targets is actually a trap trap.

In the American trap game the trap is housed in a structure measuring about eight feet square and six feet high, with about half of the height being underground. When the gunner calls "pull," the referee or puller activates the trap machine by pushing the button attached to the electrical cord; the targets emerge from the house in any direction within a radius of forty-four degrees. The trap action, that is, the swing of the metal arm, causes the target to rotate as it flies in a horizontal position with a starting velocity of about forty miles an hour and reaching a distance of about fifty yards.

The charge of shot that emerges from the gun barrel weighs 1⅛ ounces and consists of about 500 hardened lead pellets, each about 0.09 inch in diameter. The shot, usually No. 7½ or No. 8 shot, starts spreading the moment it leaves the muzzle of the gun. At forty yards, the shot spread

6

Typical American Trap shooting scene: five men at stations with a referee and puller in the rear.

encompasses a circular area about thirty inches in diameter, with some stray pellets scattered beyond that circle. Targets are generally hit between thirty and forty yards from the gun, depending on the shooter's style and the distance he or she is standing from the trap house. In most trapshooting events the participants are stationed sixteen yards from the house. In handicap events, however, the shooter may shoot from a maximum of twenty-seven yards. The shooting is done from five adjacent positions in a crescent-shaped formation. A target is scored, usually called "dead," if a piece or pieces fall from it or if it is completely shattered or "powdered." If no piece is broken off by a pellet the target is considered a miss or "lost."

A round of trap consists of twenty-five shots (one box of shells). Shooting is done in rotation with the person in Number 1 position firing first. Each shooter fires at an individual target. When each participant has fired five shots from a particular station on the crescent, all move one station to the right until each member of the squad has fired five shots from each of the five positions. Beginners usually score anywhere from five to ten hits depending upon their natural ability and the amount of instruction they have received. Good shooters will consistently score twenty-one or more. Experts are disappointed if they don't smash twenty-five straight.

7

TRAP DOUBLES

In the game of "trap doubles," which was first incorporated into tournament shooting in 1911, two targets are in the air at the same time. The gunner tries to hit them both, using two fast swinging shots. It is not extraordinarily difficult to smash both birds. In the skeet game, in fact, doubles are a regular part of the course. Still, trap doubles shooters are scarce. The reason, according to the authors of trapshooting books and articles, is that the game is thought to be much more difficult than singles trap. From my observations, however, it is apparent that comparatively few trap shooters indulge in doubles simply because a round is twice as expensive as singles and lasts only one-half the time.

Trap doubles are shot in strings of twenty-five or fifty pairs. That means that two boxes of shells are consumed to every one exploded in trap singles. Shooters who come to the trap field and club house to spend the morning or afternoon will be done shooting before they're really ready to go home— rather like the trout fisherman who plans to fish all morning, catches his limit of trout within an hour, and then is obliged by club rules to leave the stream. Besides, in trap, as in all clay target games, there is more involved in the activity than just the shooting. Shooters, whether their goals are highly competitive or just recreational, enjoy talking about the round completed, giving excuses for their misses, and offering advice to partners who missed. Sociability is involved.

Notwithstanding the relatively few numbers of participants in trap doubles, the game is a good one. I especially enjoy a few rounds just before the hunting season starts, because it loosens me up from the more precise trap and skeet birds. Occasionally I also "treat" my trap and skeet teams to a round of doubles for a bit of relaxation after a few days of serious practice. It is a perfect game to include in a "field day" shoot, where fun-games and picnics are programmed. And to those trap shooters who don't mind the extra cost I highly recommend trap doubles as an exciting and challenging game.

The angle at which the target will emerge in regular sixteen-yard trap is not known to the shooter. In trap doubles, however, the gunner has the advantage of knowing the direction of the flying targets, the trap being set to heave out the clays to the extreme left and extreme right. In other words, the trap angles are fixed so that the two targets travel straightaway from stations 1 and 5. As in singles trapshooting, each contestant takes a turn at all five stations, but in trap doubles he gets ten shots at each station instead of five.

HANDICAP TRAP

The principles of the handicap in trap are the same as those that apply in golf and other sporting games: they are designed to equalize participants of different abilities. In trap, shooting distance provides the handicap. Good shooters are bumped farther and farther away from the traphouse, up to the point where their advantage over the less accomplished shooters disappears.

Handicap distances start at eighteen yards and extend to twenty-seven yards. In popular terminology, involving "hotshot" shooters, the twenty-seven yard marker is known as "shooting from the fence."

Under the Amateur Trap Association's system an individual's handicap is decided by committees within the association. "Known ability" is determined on the basis of handicap and sixteen-yard averages and/or scores in both registered and non-registered shoots. New shooters qualifying for a "Permanent Card" must shoot 1,500 targets of either sixteen yards or handicap or a combination of both. All targets recorded must have been shot within the current year and/or the previous three years. Any shooter interested in the trapshooting handicap system should join the Amateur Trapshooting Association (see Appendix E for address). He will receive a copy of the association's "Official Trapshooting Rules," which explain the fine points in detail.

Handicap Trap. Note that shooters are at maximum handicap post at twenty-seven yards.

The following classification table demonstrates the placement of shooters of various abilities:

Class	Average at 16 yards	Handicap
AA	96.5% and over	24 to 27 yards
A	94% and under 96.5%	22 or 23 yards
B	91% and under 94%	20 or 21 yards
C	88% and under 91%	18 or 19 yards
D	Under 88%	16 yards

Although the official handicap system is controlled by the ATA, many clubs prefer to use their own handicap rules for their local unregistered shoots. The most popular alternative method is to handicap the shooter a given number of birds considering his previous average. For example, a shooter who hits 96 of 100 targets would be handicapped 12 points. If he or she scores 80 the handicap is 20; at 70 it is 28 points, and at 60 it is 38 points. Obviously, the less proficient the shooter the smaller the percentage of his handicap, and the better the shooter the greater the handicap.

INTERNATIONAL CLAY PIGEON

International Clay Pigeon, also known as International Trap or Olympic-style Trap, differs drastically from American trap. Six shooters rotate through the five stations as opposed to five shooters in American trap. The great difference between the two systems is that in the Olympic-style a fifteen-trap ground level installation, called the Olympic trench, is used. The five shooters on the straight line (not crescent-shaped as in American trap) stand sixteen meters back from the straight line of traps. Targets fly a minimum of 70 meters or about 77 yards (about 50 yards in American trap), with extreme angles and heights prevailing. Instead of one shot at each target, two shots are permitted. The bird is scored "dead" whether hit by the first or second shot.

The six-man squad changes stations after each shot, with one man always walking from Station 5 to Station 1 while the other participants shoot. A round of twenty-five is shot as one event.

In the early days of U.S. involvement in international trap (prior to World War II), only a handful of wealthy individuals were able to participate—the live pigeon shooters, again. Skeet had not yet become such a universally accepted sport. Even today skeet is not as popular as trap on the international level.

As a consequence of the United States' poor showings in the World Championships of 1954 (at Caracas, Venezuela) and 1958 (in Moscow), the Na-

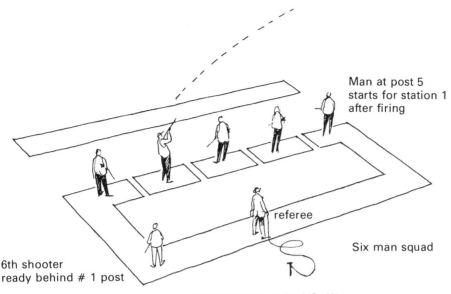

Man at post 5
starts for station 1
after firing

referee

Six man squad

6th shooter
ready behind # 1 post

INTERNATIONAL CLAY PIGEON

The International Clay Pigeon trap house roof is on an equal level with the shooting posts. The house holds 15 fixed type traps. The machines are separated about 40 inches apart in groups of three ahead of each shooting post or station. The center trap of each group is adjusted to throw targets within an area 15 degrees right or left of its center line. The left trap throws within an area straight forward to 45 degrees to right and the right machine throws within an area opposite that of the left trap. The machines are individually adjusted so that at a point 33 feet from the machine the target rises at a minimum elevation of 40 inches above the trap house roof up to a maximum of 13 feet. The shooting posts are arranged in a straight line 19.5 yards to the rear of the centers of the traps. Two shots may be fired at each target. The target can be released from any one of the three targets in front of the shooter because the machines are controlled by an electronic selector.

tional Rifle Association, in conjunction with the U.S. Army Marksmanship Training Unit (USAMTU) at Fort Benning, Georgia, began a concentrated effort to develop international skeet and clay pigeon shooters.

With the continued help of the armed forces, particularly the USAMTU, the nucleus of the U.S. international shotgun program was developed. Eventually, the NRA inaugurated the annual U.S. International Shooting Championships. The growth in participation, in spite of the "invitation" system, has been outstanding. In addition, to help attract more shotgun shooters to the international sport, the NRA began sponsoring and supporting teams to world championships in which the U.S. had never before participated.

Today there are fewer then a dozen Olympic-style fifteen-trap facilities in North America. The entire involvement in International trap is too expensive, which is the main reason why interest in the Modified Clay Pigeon game is increasing. The first two official fifteen-trap fields in the U.S. were installed at military bases: at Fort Benning, and in San Antonio, Texas. The first private Olympic-trap installation in North America was constructed at Hamilton Gun Club in Vinemount, Ontario.

International Clay Pigeon events can be scheduled in any registered shoot in the U.S. or Canada upon application to the ATA.

MODIFIED CLAY PIGEON

The trap game called "Modified Clay Pigeon" is known by several other names as well: "NRA International Clay Pigeon," "NRA Modified Clay Pigeon," "ISU Automatic Trap," and "UIT Automatic Trap." The "ISU" stands for International Shooting Union, and the "UIT" for the Union International de Tir.

Modified Clay Pigeon has been instituted in the world of flying target shooting to encourage International or Olympic-type shooting. In this game the trap houses used in American Trap shooting are suitable provided the roof of the trap pit is not higher than thirty-four inches above the level of Station 3. International Clay Pigeon or International Trap (explained elsewhere) requires an expensive fifteen-trap ground-level installation, and very few contraptions of such magnitude are found in the United States. Therefore, not many trap enthusiasts are participating in International Trap.

Although Olympic trap has been a part of the Olympic Games and World Championships almost from the beginning, it has had its ups and downs. It was dropped from the Olympics for a period of time because of the specter of "professionalism" due to the large number of live pigeon shooters who participated. Following World War II it was readmitted to the World Championships and Olympic Games. The Olympic trench has never been added to the Pan American Games program for two major reasons: trap is not as popular among the Latin-Americans as skeet and the cost of an Olympic 15-trap trench is not acceptable to the host countries. Michael Tipa of the NRA was therefore prompted to develop the "modification" for the Winchester trap and worked hard on having the Automatic Trap Game adopted by the International Shooting Union. Tipa's efforts came to fruition in 1962, when the Amateur Trapshooting Association began registering Modified Clay Pigeon. In Tipa's words: "This Modified Clay Pigeon is now official for all games and championships except the Olympics and World Championships. This is also about to be changed."

The history of the Modified Clay Pigeon game gives the participant a

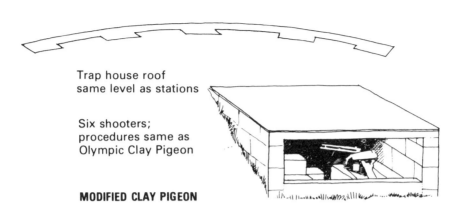

Trap house roof
same level as stations

Six shooters;
procedures same as
Olympic Clay Pigeon

MODIFIED CLAY PIGEON

In Modified Clay Pigeon the shooters are positioned one at each of five stations with the sixth participant placed towards the rear of the lane of Station 1 and ready to move onto that station. The squad rotates after each shot. Two shots may be fired at each target.

better understanding of the importance of this event, but the new shooter wants to know exactly what this type of trapshooting involves.

Although an American trap house may be used, a house with its top at ground level is preferable, for it more closely meets the requirements of an International trap facility. The trap house is equipped with a single multi-oscillating (vertical and horizontal) mechanical, or electrically operated trap. It may be manually or automatically loaded. The trap must throw targets at random and continuously changing angles and elevations within limits designated by the official rules.

Firing is normally executed by squads of six shooters. Smaller groups may participate, but for safety reasons there should be no more than six in a squad. The procedures for shooting Modified Clay Pigeon are the same as for Olympic or International Clay Pigeon. One shooter is positioned at each of the five shooting stations with the sixth participant placed towards the rear of the lane of station one and ready to move onto station one. The squad rotates after each shot. After the shooter on No. 1 station has shot his target, he or she prepares to move onto station No. 2, as soon as the shooter has fired on that station. The shooter from No. 2 moves to station 3 in a like manner after No. 3 has fired at his regular target, and so on. When the shooter on station 5 has shot his target, he or she will immediately proceed as standby to station No. 1 to continue the cycle until all shooters have shot at 25 targets. Two shots may be fired at each target.

WHAT IS SKEET?

Skeet is similar to trapshooting in that the game involves flying targets shot at with shotguns. The targets are exactly the same as those used in the trap games, that is, they resemble an inverted saucer about an inch deep, about four inches in diameter, and not quite a quarter inch thick. The brittle target breaks when hit by a shot-shell pellet. The difference is in the machine that propels the skeet target. The skeet trap throws targets in a constant or fixed pattern of flight, whereas the machine involved in trapshooting oscillates back and forth and throws the targets at angles unknown to the shooter until they emerge from the trap house. The other major difference separating the two games is that in American trap only one house, centered sixteen yards from the line of shooters, is involved. In skeet, two trap houses are used, a high house and a low house. The high house is situated at the left end of a semi-circle that contains seven of the game's eight stations; the low house is at the right end of this "half-clock" arrangement.

Skeet is a more sociable game than trapshooting. In trap, each contestant in the squad stands at an individual station, whereas in skeet one person shoots from a station while the other members of the squad wait their turn. In skeet it is easier for the squad members to observe each other's shots, and with eight stations to provide a greater variety of target flight, including doubles at four stations, there is much opportunity for the shooters to make excuses for missed targets and to criticize their friends' shooting. Generally, serious trap and skeet shooters stay with one game. Nevertheless, some of the world's best shooters do equally well at both games. The problem of becoming competent in both events is the time factor. To be a good shot requires practice. Field time, as well as personal time, make it mandatory that a serious shooter choose to concentrate on one game.

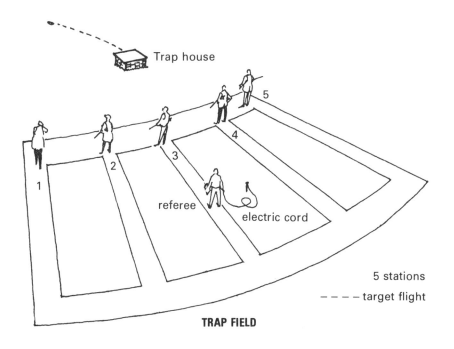

Trap house

5

4

3

2

1

referee

electric cord

5 stations

– – – – target flight

TRAP FIELD

The difference between the trap field (above) and the skeet field (below).

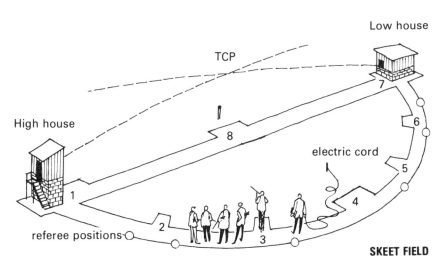

Low house

TCP

High house

7

6

8

5

electric cord

1

4

referee positions

2

3

SKEET FIELD

8 stations   Five man squad   TCP – target crossing point   – – – – target flight

15

The National Skeet Shooting Association (NSSA) is the parent body for official skeet events in the United States. It also has an international division for shooters participating under the rules used in international competition. The regulations for international or Olympic-style skeet are set by the International Shooting Union (UIT), with headquarters in West Germany.

The two standard skeet games are: American Skeet and International Skeet.

HISTORY OF SKEET

Compared to England's live-bird trapshooting activities in the late 1800's, skeet is a relatively new flying target game. And although Charles Portlock of Boston influenced the movement from live-bird to target trapshooting in America in 1866, the skeet game was not invented until 1920.

At that time, many hunters indulged in pre-season trapshooting practice in hopes of improving their bird shooting. Charles Davies of Andover, Massachusetts, a retired Boston business man, was one such ardent shooter. He became dissatisfied with the practice sessions because the crossing and incoming shots of bird shooting were absent. Consequently, he set out to devise a trap system that would more closely resemble real bird flight. Davies owned the Glen Rock Kennels, and it was on these grounds that, with the assistance of his son, Henry, and Henry's friend, Bill Foster, he began using hand traps to throw targets from different angles. Their enthusiasm grew with each innovation until they decided to develop a shooting game that would provide practice for most of the hunting shots.

They tried and discarded many plans, and finally came up with one that was satisfactory. The field was laid out in a circle with a twenty-five yard radius with twelve positions identified on the circumference, similar to a clock face. The trap was located at the head (Position 12) of the circle so that it could propel the targets towards Station 6. Starting at Station 12, each shooter fired two shots from each of the stations. The last shell remaining in the original box of twenty-five was used at the center of the circle to shoot the incoming target released from Station 12.

In 1923, Davies and his associates reduced the radius of the circle to twenty yards. Then, the experimenters ran into trouble. A neighbor started a chicken business and built ten houses in the adjacent lot facing Stations 7 to 11. Consequently, one half of the circle had to be abandoned. The change prompted the placement of a second trap, this one at the "6 o'clock" station. The stations were renumbered, 6 became 1, 12 became 7, and so on. The scheme now contained seven stations in the semi-circle, with the eighth at midfield. This is the way the stations are situated today in the modern skeet field. By adding the second trap the same target angles were presented in the semi-circle that were offered in the previous full circle plan. Next, Davies and his crew realized that because both traps were operated from ground level, certain angles of birds on the wing were not presented because the targets were not flying out at proper height. In other words, all the targets were rising. Therefore, a trap was secured to an elm tree trunk that was cut about 15 feet above ground. To further simulate hunting situations four sets of doubles were added.

Foster recognized the general appeal of this shooting game as a competitive sport and proceeded to work out a set of rules to govern the activity. He then wrote an article giving an account of the new game. It appeared in February 1926, in issues of both the *National Sportsman* and *Hunting and Fishing* magazines, along with the announcement of a national contest that offered a prize of $100.00 to the person whose name for the new game was accepted. About 10,000 entries were recorded in the contest. The lucky winner was Mrs. Gertrude Hurlbutt of Dayton, Montana. Her offering was "skeet," an old Scandinavian word meaning "shoot." Because of the wide national publicity given to the new shooting game, fields were soon cropping up all over the country.

The only book that I could find before World War II dealing with skeet was written by Bob Nichols, who in the 1920's was the skeet and shooting editor of *Field and Stream*. In 1926 he and a small group of shooters living in the New York suburban area started the Valhalla Skeet Club—the third skeet club organized in the United States. His book, titled *Skeet and How to Shoot It*, was published in 1939. The book still makes enjoyable reading. Especially delightful is an account of early skeet that bears on the history of this great game. It is worth introducing here.

Compared with the modern Skeet club, we were a motley crew back there in 1926. Our equipment was almost Spartan in its crude simplicity. Two flimsy traps threw the targets, one mounted on a rickety platform 10 feet above ground, the other slightly above ground level. The traps were entirely exposed, enclosed by no such structure as the modern trap house, and the trap loader was protected only by a sheet of corrugated iron nailed up in front of him. Incidentally, we took turns at functioning as "trap boys." Also, the trap loader was the puller. There was no central control even of the hand-operated type, let alone [an] electrically operated [one] with a timing device. Each club member who happened to be functioning as a "trap boy" at the moment, loaded and pulled at the shooter's command. One of the curious handdowns from that day to this is that many Skeet shooters still call "Pull" for the hi-trap target and "Mark" for the lo-trap target. It was necessary, of course, to have two different calls back in 1926. This was the only way the "trap boys" could understand which target was meant to be thrown.

The Skeet field of that day and on up until ten years later, in the summer of 1936, was slightly different from the layout we use today. The trap houses, facing each other, were 40 yards apart, just the same as today. Station 8 was located midway between the two traps, also the same. Thus, stations 1, 7 and 8 have remained the same since the beginning of the game. Stations 2, 3, 4, 5 and 6 have been changed. Originally these stations were located equi-distant from each other on the arc of a semi-circle swung on a 20-yard radius from station 8. Today, these shooting stations have been moved inward, and the crossing-point of target flight has been moved outward. Today, the crossing-point of target flight has been moved out 6 yards beyond station 8. And the shooting stations from 2 to 6 are now located equi-distant from each other on an arc swung from the crossing-point of target flight on a 21-yard radius. Thus, instead of the targets being thrown directly over the trap houses, on a line between station 1 and station 7, they are now thrown at an outward angle.

How and why the game was changed to "Angle" Skeet may be interesting to the reader. The idea was first brought to the author's attention by Mr. Field White of the Poly Choke Company in the summer of 1935. It was acknowledged that shooters were constantly exposed to a shower of shattered target fragments under the field lay-out of the old game, when shooting at stations 1, 7 and 8. A change in target line of flight to a pronounced outward angle would remove this hazard.

It was also suggested that with targets thrown at an outward angle, instead of on a straight line between the two trap houses, it would then be possible to locate a series of Skeet fields in a straight "down-the-line" lay-out. This would not only save space, but would also speed up the movement of shooters from one field to another in our larger state, regional and national matches. Owing to the fact that Skeet targets are shot in practically opposite directions, this matter of providing for sufficient space and safety area in laying out Skeet fields has always been a problem . . .

We were immediately struck by the significance of the proposed change and strongly suggested in the Skeet Department of *Field & Stream* that such a change be made in the standard Skeet lay-out. The idea was received with no great warmth at the moment, primarily because the Skeet game at that time was entirely under the control of a rival sporting magazine publisher.

Subsequent articles, however, stressing the safety features of the new proposed lay-out eventually got results. In the summer of 1936, at the Great Eastern Championships at Lordship, Conn., so-called "Angle" Skeet was initiated. In the National matches, following in September of that year, "Angle" Skeet became the official game. At that time we referred to the old game as "Shuttle" Skeet. However, both terms of distinction have now faded out and the official game today, with targets thrown at an outward angle, is simply Skeet.

Because the skeet game simulated wild bird shooting with no closed seasons involved, and because of the accompanying social aspects of clubs and club houses, the sport grew rapidly in popularity across the nation. Consequently, the shooters, looking for a guiding body, welcomed the formation of the National Skeet Shooting Association and its first national championship, which was held at Cleveland, Ohio, August 16-31, 1935. The number of persons taking part in the 12-gauge event was 113, a surprisingly high figure. The national championship was rotated annually around the country—St. Louis, Detroit, Tulsa, San Francisco, Syracuse and Indianapolis. The last shoot under the original association was held in Syracuse in 1942. With the outbreak of World War II the championship came to an end and civilian skeet became practically non-existent. Most of the participants went off to war, ammunition and equipment became unavailable, and gun clubs closed shop.

Skeet did not die out completely during the war. In fact, in some respects it received a boost. The military recognized the value of skeet in training personnel to lead moving targets. Consequently, thousands of men were introduced to the shotgun and the game of skeet. The Army Air Force especially encouraged the activity. And I, in 1942, in the early days of my Air Force training, took immediate advantage of the situation and became a member of the base team stationed in Georgia. Not only was it pleasurable to be required to shoot skeet as part of the Air Force training, but it was doubly enjoyable because we could shoot as much as we pleased in the off duty hours with absolutely no cost!

With the end of the war the present National Skeet Shooting Association was organized and incorporated in December 1946. The National Rifle Association played a leading role in the resurgence of the NSSA by financing a substantial, no interest loan. The National Championship was reinstituted at Indianapolis and has been held annually ever since.

The original headquarters for the Association was situated in Washington, D.C. Then it was moved to Dallas, Texas. Dallas was designated as the permanent home for the Association, including the national tournament. The permanent home policy was abolished in 1952 and the tournament's name was changed to "World Championships" and held in various fields around the country. In 1973 the Association's headquarters was moved to the National Gun Club in San Antonio, Texas. I had the valuable experience of observing the step by step construction of this facility, formerly the Texas International Gun Club, in the company of my good and long-time friend Larry Sheerin of San Antonio. Larry was the leader of the small group of ardent skeet shooters who financed and masterminded the origin and construction of this magnificent gun club.

Today, the game of skeet is recognized as a major sport nationally and internationally. It is highly regarded as a recreational pastime as well as a

19

competitive pursuit. About 20,000 shooters are members of the NSSA, and many thousands more are either members of local gun clubs or participate without having any official affiliation. Although the 12-gauge event is usually the dominant part of skeet matches and tournaments, the additional competitions in the 20 gauge, 28 gauge and the .410 bore draw much attention.

AMERICAN SKEET

Skeet, also referred to as American skeet when distinguishing the game from International skeet, takes place on a field laid out approximately in a semi-circle, with eight stations for shooting. Seven stations are situated at equal distances from one another, along the perimeter of the field with the eighth in the middle of the line between Stations 1 and 7. Station 1 is positioned at the left side of the field directly by the "high house" where the high targets emerge, and Station 7 is by the "low house" where the rising targets are thrown at the other end of the semi-circle. Although the flight pattern of the targets remains constant the angle of the targets varies because the shooter changes positions as the squad moves from one station to the next.

Five shooters make up a squad. A round of skeet for each shooter consists of twenty-five shots. Each participant shoots at a high house and a low house target at each station. Doubles, where targets from both houses fly out simultaneously, are shot from Stations 1, 2, 6, and 7. The extra or twenty-fifth shot is called "optional." The option shot is used as a repeat of the first miss. If the shooter hits all of the first twenty-four targets, the option is then taken as a second shot at low house station eight. The correct procedure is as follows: the first shooter takes his position at Station 1 and shoots at first the high house target and then the low house target. He remains on station and then shoots the doubles. The second shooter takes the same shots and is followed by the rest of the squad in turn. When all members of the squad have shot at Station 1, the first shooter proceeds to Station 2 and shoots at singles high and low and remains on station to shoot doubles. The same steps are followed by the other participants. Next the squad moves to Station 3 where only singles are shot, first the high and then the low. The same procedure is followed at Stations 4 and 5. Stations 6 and 7 are repeats of Stations 1 and 2—first the singles, low house and high house and then doubles. In doubles at Stations 6 and 7 the low house target is always shot first. At Station 8 the first shooter in the squad line-up shoots at the high house target and is followed by the others in turn. The same procedure is employed when shooting the low house target at the same station.

A scorer or referee releases the target when the shooter calls "pull." Usually, one person acts as scorer and referee. In formal matches and tournaments an effort is made to supply a scorer to mark the score sheet and a referee to push the release button on the electric extension cord that activates the trap or target throwing machine. The referee's word on the skeet field is law.

The majority of shooters use a 12-gauge gun to shoot skeet. In many tournaments, however, there are events for guns of four sizes: the .410, 28, 20 and 12 gauge. In recreational shooting the participant may shoot a round or two. Tournament events usually require one hundred or more shots per shooter. Beginners in skeet shooting usually break about six or seven targets in one round. Intermediate shooters will hit from twelve to sixteen. Good gunners will usually score between eighteen and twenty-two. Experts will have sleepless nights if they don't disintegrate at least twenty-three out of the twenty-five targets.

INTERNATIONAL SKEET

International skeet is a clay target game enjoyed by thousands of shooters throughout Europe and elsewhere abroad. It is one of the shooting events regularly scheduled in the Olympic Games, as well as being included in other World Championship events. In the United States it does not come close to reaching the popularity of American skeet, although interest in this Olympic-type clay target game is increasing rapidly.

What is the difference between International skeet and American skeet? The standard field layout is the same, but three basic requirements distinguish the Olympic-type game from the American version. First, the shooter is required to start from a low gun position; instead of mounting the gun to the shoulder he must hold the gun in a way that some part of the gun butt reaches the top of the pelvic bone. In other words, some part of the gun butt must be seen below the elbow when viewed from the side by the presiding official. Secondly, the clay targets have to be thrown to seventy-two yards—twelve yards farther than in American skeet. Consequently, they fly faster and their composition is harder (in order to prevent them from breaking when heaved from the cranked-up machine). Thirdly, a variable target may emerge from the trap house at any time up to three seconds.

Since skeet originated in America, why has the form of the game changed in Europe? Actually, International-type skeet has not changed as much from the prototype game as it may appear. Originally, skeet was shot with the gun held in the low position when the shooter was ready on station. There was also an indefinite time release after the shooter called for the bird. To illustrate this point I include the following quote taken from the first skeet "gun position" rule approved by the National Skeet Shooting Association, effective January 1, 1931:

The shooter shall not raise his gun to his shoulder to shoot until the target is seen in the air. When ready to shoot he shall take his position at the shooting station with his gun in an informal field position. He shall then order the target. The puller shall release the target at any time after the order is heard, during an indefinite period of about five seconds. The referee shall count any target as lost where the shooter places his gun butt on his shoulder to shoot before the target appears.

The "informal field position" gun rule was confusing and caused bickering among shooters and between shooters and referees whenever a participant raised "the gun closer to shoulder." Referees were also put in the awkward position of having to make "judgement calls" or personal interpretations about the proper field position of a gun. Consequently, the NSSA first modified and then eliminated both the low gun position and the detained target release. On the other hand, the Europeans, who adopted the skeet game from us in the middle 1930's, retained the "informal field game position" and cut the target delay to three seconds.

Over the years, the format, that is the station to station sequence in shooting, has remained the same in both games. In tournaments, the order in which the gunners shoot is determined by lot, and each squad shoots only twenty-five targets at a time, spreading the shooting over an entire day. However, as attendance grew at international skeet tournaments, it became apparent that squads were taking too much time to complete their rounds. Too many shooters were "fiddling around" on station before calling for the bird. Consequently, the International Shooting Union published revised rules, which became effective January 1, 1977. The shooter was now required to load the gun and call for the target within fifteen seconds. The number of shooters per squad was increased to six, the shooting sequence was changed and the "optional" shot was eliminated.

An announcement released by Michael Tipa, chairman of the U.I.T. Technical Committee, spelled out the official changes in International Skeet Rules:

1. In all UIT sanctioned competition, skeet squads will be formed with six (6) individuals. Squads may shoot with less than six members when the drawing of lots does not permit an even distribution.

2. A time limit of 15 seconds is established for loading and preparation on the station. Each shooter must step onto his station, take his position, load his gun and call for his target within 15 seconds.

3. The shooter MUST load two (2) cartridges for singles targets on stations 2, 3, 4, 5, and 6. On station 8 he must load only ONE cartridge to shoot at the target from each house.

22

4. SEQUENCE OF SHOOTING

Station			
One	-	1 Single from High house	+ one pair doubles
Two	-	2 Singles (1 from Hi & 1 from Low)	+ one pair doubles
Three	-	2 Singles (1 from Hi & 1 from Low)	+ one pair doubles
Four	-	2 Singles (1 from Hi & 1 from Low)	+ *NO DOUBLES*
Five	-	2 Singles (1 from Hi & 1 from Low)	+ one pair doubles
Six	-	2 Singles (1 from Hi & 1 from Low)	+ one pair doubles
Seven	-	*NO SINGLES* *ONLY*	+ one pair doubles
Eight	-	1 Single from High house and 1 Single from Low house	

NOTE: Shooters will move from station 7 and line up in order behind the field referee on a line between stations 8 and 4.

The first shooter takes his position on station 8 in the normal manner, loading *ONE* cartridge only, shooting at the target from the High house then, turning in a clockwise direction (rotating to the right) take his position for the Low house, load *ONE* cartridge and shoot at a target from the Low house. Each succeeding shooter follows the same procedure.

There is no longer an "optional" shot. This is dispensed with by shooting the single target from the High house on station 1.

Through a council, the International Shooting Union, supported by many countries, initiates and enforces the "Regulations for Skeet Shooting." The leading proponent of developing International skeet in the United States is the International and Shotgun Department of the National Rifle Association.

As mentioned previously, International skeet is nowhere near as popular in the United States as American skeet. There are signs, however, that this "off-the-hip" type of skeet has been attracting more shooters, especially the younger ones. For example, in the 1977 National Intercollegiate Championships held in Omaha, Nebraska, twenty-three colleges and universities participated in American skeet and eighteen of them also took part in the international game.

Is International skeet less popular because it is a more difficult game? Not necessarily. If a person concentrates on the Olympic game he will become proficient at it. Generally, while doing so, his American skeet scores will drop. Perhaps the shooting relationship between American skeet and International skeet is similar to that between trap and skeet. If a shooter desires to become truly proficient at shooting any one of these events his efforts should be expended on the one game of his choice. Another reason why American skeet is vastly more popular than Olympic-style is simply because it has been in existence in the United States for many more years. Furthermore, the facilities for shooting Olympic-style are comparatively few. True, the shooter can practice the low gun position, and the referee can restrain his pull of the target for up to three seconds, but the pinch comes with the target throwing machines. The machines used at nearly all skeet fields are not geared to throw International skeet targets. First, the club manager does not favor cranking-up the American skeet machine because it is a nuisance to him. And second, his reluctance to "beef up" the mechanism to throw faster targets is well founded in the fact that the motor is not geared to pull a spring set heavy enough to throw the target the extra distance required for the International game. The change produces an undue strain on the equipment, and the housing on the trap itself may break. Another obvious problem is squadding. A regular skeet shooter at any field may enter into a scheduled squad that has an opening, but an International skeet devotee cannot mix into such a group. Special time and field arrangements have to be made for him and the other followers of his game if the shooting grounds do not possess an Olympic-type skeet facility. Efforts to encourage more shooters to participate in the challenging International game will therefore be frustrated until more fields include permanent Olympic-style skeet fields.

2 - The Competitions

THE EVENTS

Competitions involving the formal trap and skeet shooting events are many and varied. They range all the way from single-day, low key, twenty-five-target shoots, run for members of the local club, to the ultimate in national, international and world championships where individual gunners fire hundreds of rounds over several days just to qualify for the finals. Some of the types of competitions are postal matches, state and regional championships, registered and non-registered shoots, tournaments sanctioned by specific associations, open-to-all tournaments, intercollegiate matches and intercollegiate national championships. There are classification and qualification shooting schemes mothered by national associations. Others are junior championships, senior championships, wheelchair tournaments for the handicapped, holiday shoots, memorial shoots, and programs that honor an individual. And then there are club leagues, industrial, individual and team leagues. The list goes on and on.

A few of the most prestigious international shotgun competitions occur in the Olympic Games, World Skeet and Clay Pigeon Championships, Pan American Games and the Confederation of Americas Championships.

In trap shooting, the Grand American is by far the most prestigious of the national tournaments. The Golden West Grand American trapshoot tournament, another famous competition, is second only to the Grand American in numbers of participants.

In skeet, some of the national events of prominence are: NSSA World Championships, the Great Eastern, Mid-West Open, Mid-America, and Great Western. Numerous other tournaments, such as the Road Runner Open hosted by the NSSA at the National Gun Club in San Antonio, Texas, and the ATA Spring Grand American held at the Phoenix Trap and Skeet Club, are held throughout the country. And most of these tournaments involve a great many shooters attracted by substantial money prizes.

To cover all the different kinds of big, national and international trap and skeet events would require a volume in itself. However, to give readers some insight into the enormous scope of the shotgun games and their importance in the world of sport, a brief review of a few of them is in order.

OLYMPIC GAMES

International shooting matches began being popular in the nineteenth century. Officials of the first modern Olympiad, the 1896 games held in Athens, Greece, encouraged this type of competition by including a few shooting contests in the program. The first formal International Rifle Shooting Championships were held in Lyon, France, the following year. The interest aroused by this competition led to the formation in 1907 of L'Union des Fédérations et Associations Nationals de Tir, the forerunner of the International Shooting Union, which today provides rules and controls the formal international shotgun games.

Target shooting as a competitive riflery sport in the United States did not take place until the formation of the National Rifle Association of America (NRA) in 1871 by a group of National Guard officers. And it was the leaders of riflery who eventually stimulated the shotgunners to be involved in the Olympics. The International Clay Pigeon event was initiated as an Olympic sport in 1952. And International Skeet followed in 1968. At the 1976 Olympics, some fifty countries took part in the International Skeet and International Clay Pigeon competitions.

MAKING THE OLYMPIC TEAM

I have asked Brad Simmons to write a few lines about making the 1979 U.S. Olympic Team in International Skeet. Brad was a member of the 1977 U.S. Team that won the World Championship in Antibes, France. During the finals of the tryouts held in St. Louis in July, Brad set new records in collegiate, men's open and world competition with a score of 390 targets hit out of 400. Just as important to me as Yale's trap and skeet coach, Brad was captain of the Yale Skeet Team that won the National Intercollegiate Championships in Omaha, Nebraska. These are Brad's words:

> In order to become a U.S. team member, one must go through two phases of tryouts, the first being at the preliminary level. The NRA sponsors ten different Zone tryouts covering five states per zone. To succeed at this level, the shooter must either (1) place in the top ten of the match, or (2) shoot a score of 180 × 200 or better. He is then entitled to apply for an invitation to the final tryouts. Once invited, the shooter must prepare to make his key performance of the year. In the case of the 1976 Olympic Team Trials, of 150 people who came to compete, only two went to the Olympics. Thus, you do not go to a U.S. Team Tryout with anything in mind but getting first place! At the 1976 Olympic Trials in Skeet and Trap, held in Pacific, Missouri, there was more pressure then I have ever

Brad Simmons, captain of the Yale skeet team and member of the U.S. Olympic International Skeet team, demonstrates the "gun butt above hip" position required for International Skeet.

experienced at a tournament—more even than the Olympics themselves. What happened to me there is proof of the old adage that there is always a chance to come back hard. I shot a 21 my first round; the shooters holding the top two places had missed fewer targets than that in three days! But I was not the only person who had been feeling the strain; I had merely gotten mine out of the way early! At the end of the twelfth round three days later, there was a four-way tie for first place—myself, Norman Svarrer, John Satterwhite, and Phil Province. The shoot-off that followed left Satterwhite and myself with 25's, Svarrer 24 and Province 23. The "Team" positions had been won.

Changes have since been made in the format of the U.S. tryouts. In 1977 the tryouts became a 400-target event. The top twenty shooters of the first 300 went on to compete on the fourth day for the last 100 targets. The best totals out of the 400 determine the final standings. However, the off-Olympic years rules allow for four-man teams to be chosen to compete in international team competition. The four places in 1977 were held by Dan Carlisle, Al Mullins, Bill Clemons and myself. Our team went to Antibes, in September of that year and won the first World Championship Gold Medal in team competition in United States history.

There are other things besides the official scores that must be considered when attempting to make a U.S. Team. These are the personal qualities that make up the shooter's edge in a head to head competition such as a United States Team tryout.

One of these qualities is *endurance*. The person who can not only withstand pressure, but last longer than the others while doing so has an edge not only in a shooting tryout, but in any high-pressure competition.

Another important personal quality in the shooting sports is the ability to *concentrate* on what you are doing rather than thinking about the kids, your job, or that blonde walking down the sidewalk behind you. In the fraction of a second it takes for your concentration to drift you've lost another target. But too many shooters try to concentrate *all* the time during a match. The good shooter is able to direct his concentration totally for the short time he needs it, and to rest in-between.

Also important in gaining a winning edge in shooting is the element of *style*. Once you learn a style and shoot it well, don't walk into a match and start changing it! You'll only prove two things: that you don't have confidence in your own style and that you are too busy thinking about changing styles to concentrate on the task at hand—breaking all of the targets! Develop your style, put your faith in it, and don't be persuaded to change it in mid-stream.

Another key ingredient in successful competition shooting is to *know the rules* of the game. Nothing destroys confidence and concentration more than having some rule called on you in a match.

When competing in any match, *don't compare scores* or keep a record of your place in the standing. Nothing you do will hurt you more in a clay pigeon sport than an overdose of confidence or a "stab" of panic.

A *very* important key to maintaining a winning edge is *being independent*. If you listen to what everyone has to say and take everyone's advice, the concentration time involved alone would draw from your attention toward the competition itself. Also, the factor of style comes into play again, for the winners in the game are the ones independent enough to follow their style and not question it. Make winning your priority, and don't let lesser issues get in the way.

The final element of gaining a winning edge in shooting is *never quitting*, no matter how many birds that you are down in a match. Personal experience has taught me this lesson. In the Olympic trials in 1976 for Skeet Shooting, I was down four targets after the first round of competition! There were 275 left to shoot, and at the end I had caught up (shooting a

28

292 out of 300). In the ensuing shoot-off with the three other men, factors such as style and concentration were a benefit to my performance. But they would not have helped one bit if I had given up after shooting a 21 in the first round. It goes back to a phrase seen on many junior high and high school football lockers—"Winners Never Quit, and Quitters Never Win!"

GRAND AMERICAN

The Grand American Handicap is the single largest participation sporting event in the world. Annually, in August, more than 4,000 trapshooters from all parts of the United States and Canada participate in this greatest of all shooting tournaments, with men, women, and children competing on equal terms for the championship. Held in Vandalia, Ohio, the Grand American trapshooting Championship is actually the national championship for the Amateur Trapshooting Association (ATA), the organization that supervises and promotes registered tournament trapshooting in the United States and Canada.

Ten days of non-stop shooting are required to complete the sixteen major championships. In order to expedite this crowded and intense competition, all of the seventy-two tournament and practice traps, strung along a mile and a half of trap fields, are put into play.

Much more is involved with the Grand American than the actual gunning. The shooting facility is the home of the ATA and the ATA Hall of Fame Museum. It is also the place where the most important of the commercial companies involved with the huge clay target shooting market maintain year-round headquarters from which they promote their products. During the great tournament the products and their makers are very much in evidence: shot shell loading machines, the finest of trap guns, the best of the stock makers and gun engravers, manufacturers of the top-grade shooting and apparel accessories. Although the actual shooting programs are extremely serious, the surrounding atmosphere is like that an annual fair.

The Grand American Handicap started in 1900 at a shooting club at the Interstate Park, Queens, Long Island, New York. The original four day tournament ran from June 12 to 15. The feature of the shoot was a one-hundred-target event at handicap distances ranging from fourteen to twenty-five yards. In recent years, it has been the custom for the stars of shooting to win the sixteen-yard events while the unknowns win the Grand American Handicap. Ned Lilly, who in 1933 at the age of seventeen, broke 199 × 200 to become the youngest North American Clay Target Champion in ATA history, presented me with a copy of *The Grand—A History of Trap Shooting*, by Jimmy Robinson and Jim Nicholas, a volume I recommend highly to anyone interested in the detailed history of this magnificent event. For specific information concerning procedures for entering the Grand, inquiries should be sent to the Amateur Trapshooting Association located at Vandalia, Ohio. *Trap and Field*, the ATA's official monthly magazine, carries a wealth of information relating not only to the Grand American, but also to other trapshooting tournaments. All shooters interested in trap shooting should join the ATA and receive this attractive and informative magazine. Annual membership is $5.00 and membership blanks are available at gun clubs and from the ATA office, Vandalia, Ohio 45377.

WORLD SKEET AND CLAY PIGEON CHAMPIONSHIPS

In 1977, a twenty-member U.S. team took part in the World Skeet and Clay Pigeon Championships held in Antibes, France. The competition, in which nearly forty countries participated, ran from September 7 to 17.

The U.S. Team, selected by the National Rifle Association (which paid all expenses), included ten skeet shooters and ten clay pigeon shooters. These were grouped in teams of four in the Open (men's), three in the Ladies, and three in the Junior divisions for skeet, with identical groupings for clay pigeon. The gunners that made this team also participated in the Championship of the Americas (Mexico City, November 1977).

In the championships the U.S. Senior Men's Team won the Gold Medal—the first gold for U.S. skeet shooters in twenty-five years. The team score was 577 out of a possible 600. France was second with 573 and Sweden finished third with 571. The world's record of 588 out of a possible 600, won by United States in Mexico City in 1973, remained unbroken as of this writing.

NSSA WORLD CHAMPIONSHIPS

This greatest of all American skeet events, sponsored by the National Skeet Shooting Association, takes place annually in the United States because it is here that nearly all of the American style skeet (gun mounted to shoulder) is practiced. Representatives from a few foreign countries do participate, however.

With some practice shooting included, it takes about a week to complete the four events, which are the .410, 28, 20 and 12 gauges competitions. Concurrent champion events or divisions are: Open champion, Runner-up Champion, Lady, Junior, Sub-junior, Collegiate, Military, Industry, Two-Man Team, and Five-Man Team. The .410, 28 and 20 gauge are one-hundred-target events. The 12-gauge event requires the shooter to fire at

250 clays. Many shooters enter all events hoping to take the High Overall Championships.

ACU-I INTERCOLLEGIATE TRAP AND SKEET CHAMPIONSHIPS

Intercollegiate trap and skeet shooting competitions are growing at a tremendous rate. Many matches, leagues and regional shoots take place during the school year. The big event, however, sponsored by the Association of College Unions—International is the Intercollegiate Championships. The Ninth Annual five-day event held in Omaha, Nebraska April 13 to 17, 1977, had 222 students representing 44 institutions from 22 states registered and competing in the four separate games.

3 - The Novelty Clay Target Games

The informal or novel clay target games do not receive as much attention as formal trap and skeet activities do. The informal or "fun" games of clay target shooting bear the same relation to trap and skeet as the game of touch football does to regular football games. We are all aware of the great number of football games that take place regularly throughout the country. But who, aside from the participants themselves, ever takes note of the innumerable touch football contests and the associated spontaneous activities of passing and catching the football?

Trap and skeet games require organization and formality, just as football does. The shooter's scores are noted on specially designed score sheets each time a round of twenty-five targets is shot. The individual's scores are also kept in club house books and sent for tabulation to regional and national associations to which the participants belong. Also, various organized shoots, matches, tournaments and championships are available to any shooter who desires formal competition. On the other hand, in a situation similar to "do it yourself" football, there are thousands of shooters who prefer to do their clay target shooting informally on their own and using their own equipment. The fact that hand traps, practice traps, and clay targets are readily obtainable at most hunting and fishing supply stores encourages shooters to try the fun shooting games. So does the fact that everyone can enjoy the sport year-round, and regardless of age or sex.

As I look back at many years of shooting experiences I realize that some of my most pleasant and memorable outings have been with my family, especially when my children, Nancy and Tom, were ten and twelve years of age. We would fill a picnic basket and spend the day by a pond and open fields of Fair Haven Heights in Connecticut. In the morning we fished for yellow perch and bullheads and in the afternoon I taught the children how to hit clay targets with a .410 shotgun while their mother loaded the portable trap and pulled the cord. In retrospect I strongly recognize that these outings proved to be an immensely valuable family activity. Through the various steps of teaching Nancy and Tom gun handling and recreational shooting,

The novelty clay target games are ideally suited as an activity for family picnics. At bottom, a hand trap.

I was able to instill in them, during their most formative years, the discipline, good manners and courtesy that I now see coming to fruition in their teen years.

Before we delve deeper into the games of informal shooting with hand traps and practice traps, it is safe to assume that some readers may not be acquainted with such mechanisms and how they are used. Therefore, a brief description is warranted at this point, even though the subject is discussed in detail in another chapter.

HAND AND PORTABLE TRAPS

Hand trap designs vary, depending on the manufacturer. Some are more elaborate than others, and consequently the price varies. Basically, the hand trap consists of a wooden, metal, or plastic handle or grip with an extension of about eight or ten inches, to which is attached the two-pronged metal device that holds the clay target. A spring holds the target firmly until the target is released. The release comes when the thrower's arm, in its swing, reaches proper momentum. The simpler hand traps have only two heavy wires to hold the target; others are arranged to harbor two or three targets within parallel tracks for throwing "doubles" and "triples." The better grade hand traps have a flexible spring that connects the handle to the target holder; the whipping action of the spring adds speed and distance to the target when cast.

The moveable or portable trap machines are also available in different designs, but their mechanics are similar. Each has a metal base to which are

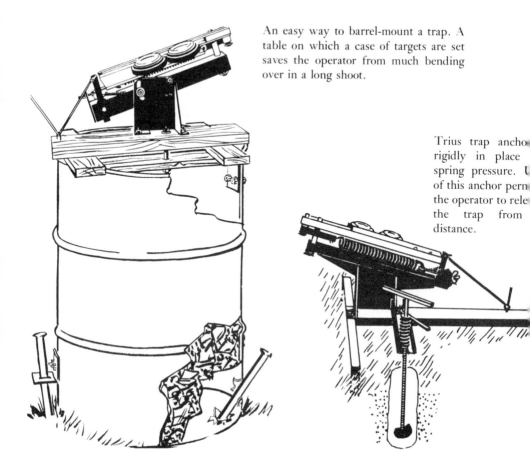

An easy way to barrel-mount a trap. A table on which a case of targets are set saves the operator from much bending over in a long shoot.

Trius trap ancho rigidly in place spring pressure. U of this anchor perm the operator to rele the trap from distance.

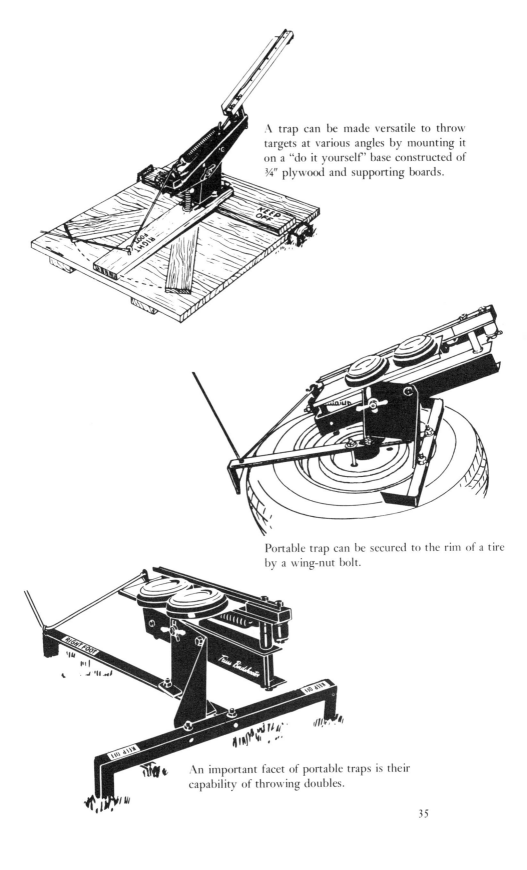

A trap can be made versatile to throw targets at various angles by mounting it on a "do it yourself" base constructed of ¾" plywood and supporting boards.

Portable trap can be secured to the rim of a tire by a wing-nut bolt.

An important facet of portable traps is their capability of throwing doubles.

attached an oblong-shaped, smooth-surfaced arm and a heavy spring. To throw a target, the arm is cocked in place, then released by means of a cord attached to the trigger. Some portable traps are equipped with "hold down" anchors which, when stuck in the ground, hold the trap rigidly in place. Others are held down by foot or mounted over a tire rim, with the base of the trap secured to the hub with a bolt. In regular shooting areas a permanent wooden base is usually constructed. And I have seen a portable trap mounted on top of a discarded oil drum. Weighted with field stones, the drum made a perfectly adequate mount.

A portable trap can be held down by foot as the operator pulls the cord.

Some models come equipped with can-throwing attachment.

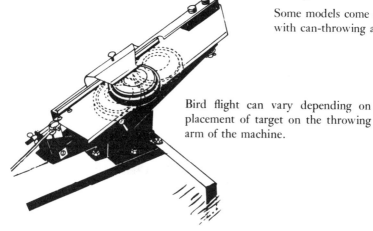

Bird flight can vary depending on placement of target on the throwing arm of the machine.

Portable traps are light in weight, most are adjustable without tools, and all can be easily transported by car. They propel double as well as single trap and skeet targets, and the targets' angles of flight and distance are adjustable. Moveable traps are available wherever guns and ammunition are sold. If the shop manager has none in stock, he will probably order one or supply the customer with the name and address of one of the companies that produces traps.

The hand trap, and then the more substantial portable or practice trap, was invented by bird hunters who, before the start of the season wished to sharpen their marksmanship by shooting at flying targets. Clay targets

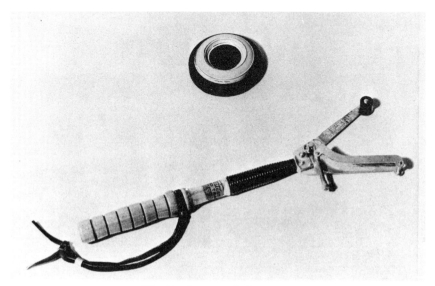

The hand trap and clay target

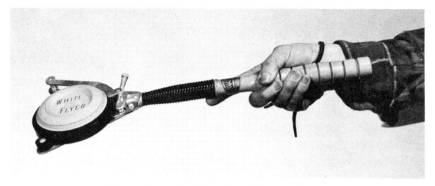

The hand trap loaded and ready to be thrown

thrown by hand were not satisfactory because their flight distances were too short. Then all sorts of contraptions were tried, such as broom handles and elastic bands cut from rubber tire tubes, but they weren't much better. When some entrepreneurs devised a home-made hand trap with handle, two prongs and a spring, manufacturers took note and started to produce an improved device. As a result, informal shotgun shooting practice became attractive to gunners.

The hand trap method of throwing the clay bird into flight is still the least expensive way to participate in clay target shooting. All you need is a case of targets and an open area where shooting is legal. Two people are needed, one to shoot and the other to toss the targets.

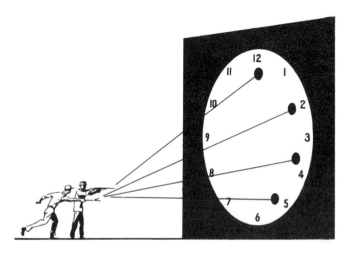

Hand trap games resemble most every type of shot that a hunter can expect in the field. With practice, a hand trap thrower can vary his tosses to afford shots very similar to the close-to-the-ground rabbit shot, the somewhat higher quail shot, the still higher but straight-flying pheasant shot, and the high-flying duck or goose shot.

There is a technique involved in heaving targets correctly, and in order to teach someone to shoot at flying targets, the thrower must be proficient at that technique. It is important for the newcomer to know in which direction the target is going to fly, but if the targets are badly thrown they will flounder out every which way, including vertically, instead of horizontally, causing the clay bird to dive suddenly to earth. Because instructions for throwing targets usually do not accompany the hand trap in the store-bought package, a few hints on proper throwing procedure would seem to be in order.

Walking Target (left): Thrower walks behind and to the side of the shooter. The thrower tries to out-fox the shooter with a high or low angle bird.

Twisting Floater (top right): A well-practiced thrower can perfect this "teaser," making the target float out lazily in front of the shooter.

Double Targets (bottom right): One thrower releases his target a little behind the other—a double deception shot for the shooter.

Most hand traps have a leather thong or strap attached at the upper end of the handle. Use of the strap is recommended. The thrower puts his hand through the loop before grasping the handle. Should the thrower lose his grip on the handle the thong, when secured around the wrist, will prevent the trap from flying out and possibly hitting the shooter. Also, if the strap is of the proper length and feels secure around the wrist, it will increase wrist support, enabling you to heave the target farther with less effort.

There are four basic directions in which to throw a target, left and right, high and low. Let us start from the beginning, using a right handed thrower. (Left handers can reverse the instruction from right to left.)

The throwing sequence can be separated into three basic operations:

1. STANCE

The legs should the positioned comfortably in the direction of the intended target flight with the left leg forward and the feet spread apart, about shoulder width, in the same position used in throwing a ball.

2. WEIGHT DISTRIBUTION

Initially, all of the body weight will rest on the back leg, remaining in that position for as long as the throwing arm is cocked behind the body in preparation for the swing. The body weight is shifted from the rear (right) leg to the forward (left) leg in one smooth flying motion at the same time the throwing arm is being swung forward. Half way through the swing, body weight should be equal on both legs. As the arm swings ahead of the body, releasing the target, all the weight should be on the front leg for a good follow through.

3. ARM POSITION

The arm is held in a "side-arm" throwing position just back of the right shoulder. The elbow, about equal level with the wrist, and extended about three-quarters of the way, should create an angle of about 135 degrees. With the wrist cocked back as far as possible, the arm is swung forward, accompanied by a strong wrist action. The arm swing is very much like the throw one uses to skip a flat stone across the water, or in fly fishing, when putting the rod into action under low hanging tree limbs.

The entire swing is kept waist high for a target flight not too high above the ground. When targets are being thrown at an average height to the extreme left or right and to all the angles in between, only the stance shifts; the arm and wrist movements remain the same. The higher the target is intended to fly, the higher the forward swing will end. But, good snappy wrist action is important regardless of the height of the flying target. With practice the thrower can become proficient at throwing high and low targets as well as fast and slow ones.

Not long after the emergence of the factory-made hand traps, gunners discovered that practicing with them was more than just preparing for the hunting season; it was fun. Because of the popularity of the hand trap, manufacturers produced a more sophisticated portable trap machine known as the practice trap. Fathers who used these traps found it much easier to introduce their sons to shooting. Today, however, family clay target shooting is no longer only a "father and son" affair. Daughters and mothers have entered the picture strongly. And nowadays, it is not unusual to see an entire family enjoying a combined shoot and picnic.

During the past decade sportsmen have given more attention than usual to the clay target games. And with the continuing decline of available hunting areas not only has individual interest in the informal, fun clay target games increased, but shooting clubs in general have incorporated "fun games" into their programs. Now, many clubs use their formal trap and skeet fields for informal games, combining parts of regular trap and skeet shooting with such games as *Grouse Walk, Duck Tower, Dove Shoot, Turkey*

Shoot, and doubles thrown from a portable trap. For example, the Yale University Trap and Skeet Club runs an Annual Clay Target Games Field Day for students, faculty, staff and alumni, that with an exciting mixture of games as well as a cook-out and an awards presentation.

The games described below are ones that have been used successfully by many organizations; some have been invented by the Yale Trap and Skeet Club or modified to meet college student interests. Any chairman, manager, or coach of shotgun shooting activities can easily modify these events or add his own ideas. The one extremely important restriction to the formulation of these games is that the chairman be a person with years of experience in gun safety. The informal shooting games are designed for fun and recreation, but the leader should maintain a severe "no nonsense" attitude. And he should insist, above all, that participants in clay target games always wear *protective eye glasses*.

TYPES OF NOVELTY GAMES

The novelty clay target games may be grouped into five categories:

1. Those that involve the portable traps, that is, hand traps and practice traps.
2. Games that take place on the trap field.
3. Games adaptable to the skeet field.
4. Games that require special facilities.
5. The "Field Day" games that may combine activities of all the previous four.

HAND TRAP GAMES

The evolution of the clay target and the availability of the inexpensive hand trap have opened unlimited possibilities for individuals and families to participate in private shooting at low cost. Hand trap games are economical, versatile, and adaptable to any terrain, provided only that a safety area of three hundred yards can be maintained. If you intend to shoot on private property be sure to obtain permission from the owner.

The arrangement for a shooting sequence or the set-up of a game will vary depending upon the individual shooters. Easy targets, thrown straight ahead should be presented to the novice. If the participants are experienced, the height and angle of the flying targets are limited only by safety factors. Obviously, the thrower should stand to one side and far enough behind the shooter to be safe and not a distraction.

Regardless of the degree of the expertise of the gunners, the efficient execution of the games will be hindered if the thrower is unable to control the direction of the target's flight. Anyone taking a turn at target throwing should first practice with the hand trap without a shooter on station. The inexperienced thrower should not be trying to master the proper arm swing and target release time when a shooter is patiently waiting for the target to appear. Before any hand trap shooting is attempted the thrower should have had enough practice heaving targets so that each throw is under control; that is, the target should fly in the direction the thrower intends it to go. If the shooter is apprehensive about the capability of the thrower the consistency of his shooting will suffer.

Although many gunners are introduced to shotgunning through the use of hand traps, the use of a stationary trap is preferable for teaching shooting, especially when teaching children. The new shooter will be nervous enough without having the added concern of not knowing which direction the target will be flying. The neophyte should first become acquainted with proper stance, gun point, shell sound and gun recoil before he starts thinking about swing and lead. It is important therefore that the targets should all be straight-aways until such time as the student is breaking them consistently. More detailed information on how to teach shooting is found in this book.

GAMES CONSIST OF TWENTY-FIVE SHOTS

In most games, the shooter is given a total of twenty-five tries, because that is the standard number of shells contained in a box. For example, if the gunners are primarily interested in a rabbit shoot, all twenty-five shots can be used at targets thrown as low as possible to the ground, or six shells can be used at each of four different heights of flying targets in order to simulate field shooting at rabbits, quail, pheasants and ducks or geese. As in skeet shooting, the twenty-fifth shell is used for an option shot, as a repeat of the first target missed.

THE NO-GUN CLAY TARGET GAME

Before discussing the various hand target games, I should mention a clay-target game that requires no gun—a game I developed during one of the Annual Field Days sponsored by the Yale Trap and Skeet Club at Yale's Outdoor Education Center. Among the scheduled events was a fly casting competition, in which the participants cast flies at a set of five targets. The targets were hoops thirty inches in diameter, each a different color and each floating in the trout pond at a different distance from the caster. If a fly fell into the hoop or touched it, the cast was called "perfect," with scores being determined by the number of direct hits and the distance of the misses from the hoop. While watching this game, it suddenly occurred to me that a similar contest might be developed as an additional event in the shooting program: a hand-trap, clay-target throwing competition. Heading for the trap and skeet area, we laid out the same colored hoops used in the fly casting game (although old bicycle tires could have been used just as well), but placed them at greater distances. The referee called out the color of the hoop that the thrower was to aim for.

As in the fly casting contest, each competitor had ten tries and started with a total of one hundred points. A throw was called perfect if the target fell no more than ten feet from the center of the hoop. If the target dropped between ten and twenty feet from center, five points were deducted. If the clay hit the ground between twenty feet and thirty feet from center, ten points were taken from the score. To measure the distances, a peg was inserted at the center of each hoop, and the referee placed a marker at the spot where each of the thrower's casts hit the ground. After the ten throws were completed, it required but a few moments to establish the score by measuring the distances between drops and center pegs. The game proved to be great fun, and helped introduce our shooters to the hand-trap method of throwing clay targets.

UPLAND GAME SHOOT

The *Rabbit Run*, *Quail Shots*, *Flying Pheasants* and *Dove Shoot* are hand-trap clay-target games that can either be treated as individual events or scored in combination in the over-all game called "Upland Game Shoot." The objective is to throw the targets so they ride at heights that will simulate the flight patterns of real, feathered game. In all four games the shooter, standing in one spot, has a try at targets heaved by the thrower in three directions: to left, straight ahead and to the right.

The *Rabbit Run* targets are cast forth as close as possible to the ground. In *Quail Shots* the targets are thrown to fly at a height of about eight feet, because quail in the wild do not fly very high when they break cover. From my pheasant shooting experiences, I judge that a hand trap clay target, coasting along at an average height of fifteen feet, is about right to imitate the live bird in the *Flying Pheasants* event. The target for the *Dove Shoot* should be thrown to fly about eighteen to twenty feet above ground.

If the combined hits of all four events are to be counted as a final score, each shooter takes four turns at the shooting station, thereby consuming twenty-four shells. The first gunner shoots two rounds (shooting left, straight ahead and right twice in succession) at the *Rabbit Run* targets. Then the other gunners take their turn at the same targets before the first contestant returns to station and shoots his next two rounds at the quail event targets. The same procedure is followed until all contestants have shot six times at each of the four-event targets. Each shooter takes his twenty-fifth or option shot as a repeat of the first target missed.

DUCK SHOOTS

PASS SHOOTING

One of the most common shots in duck shooting, often referred to as a "pass shot" or "pass shooting" is when ducks do not intend to stool, that is, to come into the decoys; instead they swing by "to take a look." Also, duck hunters off the New England coast operate from rocks along the shore or from small islands not too far distant from shore. Scoters are quarry in this type of rock shooting, but more often than not, these ducks don't decoy, especially later in the season when they become rock shy. Nevertheless, as they swing by in range, but at tremendous speed, these big, hardy birds offer challenging targets to the gunner. Unquestionably, the main reason for missed shots is because the hunter does not lead the bird far enough. Whether the gunner is a duck shooter practicing "lead" for the upcoming season or whether he is interested only in hitting clay targets, the game of Pass Shooting is a good one.

PASSING DUCKS

Three persons are best for the Passing Ducks shoot. The gunner takes a stand in line with two throwers, one on each side. The distances between gunner and thrower should be changed after each round and the angle of the flying targets should also be increased making them more difficult to hit. If the shooters wish, a box of shells may be consumed at this exercise. For example, each gunner shoots at a right and left target alternately. The second and third time the right and left targets are shot, from the same station, their flying height is increased. After each shooter has shot at six targets, three from each side, the throwers move further away, but equidistant, from the shooting station. If the throwing action takes place from four different distances on each side of the shooter, twenty-four shells will have been used, with the twenty-fifth used as a repeat of the first target missed.

DUCKS DECOYING

With ideal conditions prevailing and the wind at the gunner's back, the ducks' final descent into the decoys will come from directly in front, that is, against the wind. The Ducks Decoying game is an attempt to have the clay targets simulate ducks swiftly dropping into the decoys. And it makes an interesting shoot because the targets are coming at the gunner and dropping down a short distance ahead.

The best way to execute this game is for the thrower to be situated atop

44

High-Flying Ducks

a cliff, clay bank or a high sand dune and, of course, far enough away from the edge so as not to be in danger of being hit by shot pellets. The gunner's position will be designated by the area in which the targets actually hit the ground. The thrower must attempt to heave the targets into the dropping zone with some degree of consistency. The gunner may move forward or backward in order to reach the desired distance for shooting.

HIGH-FLYING DUCKS

In hunting, it often happens that ducks will come flying high and fast past the gunner. Most often such flights occur at dusk when the birds travel, without pause, from feeding areas to the marshes and ponds where they spend the night. In such cases, the ducks have no intention of decoying, but when approaching the area of descent, they will often fly within gun range. At such times, the shooter, crouching behind a bush or in a ditch, experiences some magnificent overhead "pass shooting," as opposed to pass shooting over decoys, when the birds come in much lower and pass in front of the gunner.

The High-flying Ducks game is much the same as the Ducks Decoying, the targets being tossed toward the shooter from the top of a clay bank, sand dune or steep hillside. However, in the duck-decoying event the targets fall in front of the shooter, whereas in the high-flying game the clays are heaved hard enough to pass at a good height over the head of the person on the shooting station.

The gunner can provide himself with another type of high pass-shooting shot by simply moving thirty or forty feet to one side and standing at a right

45

angle to the path of the flying targets. A fast swing and a substantial lead of four feet or more is then necessary to knock down the targets.

If a scoring game is desired, three parts can be included in the High-flying or High-passing Ducks game. Each gunner in turn shoots six targets at each of four stations. The twenty-fifth shell or option shot is used as a repeat of the first target missed. Shooting Stations 1 and 2 are located in a line perpendicular to the cliff so that the targets pass overhead. The first station should be positioned a convenient distance away from the base of the cliff, the second station about thirty or forty feet further back. Station 3 could be located thirty or forty feet to the left of Station 2, while Station 4 might be a similar distance to the right of Station 2.

DUCK BLIND SHOTS

As an explanation for non-hunters: a duck blind is a structure intended to conceal the gunners when ducks, attracted by decoys bobbing on the water, fly overhead. The blind is usually constructed of materials that will blend in with the surrounding landscape.

Clay target shooting from a duck blind is intended for water-side shooting and it can be practiced from a regular hunting blind. Duck hunters wouldn't be throwing clay targets when there was a possibility that real ducks would be flying around. Bright, sun shiny mid-days, and bluebird days when not a blade of grass is stirring is the time to break the monotony by banging away at some clays tossed out by hand traps. But the gunner need not necessarily wait until the hunting season to enjoy this type of waterside shooting. And a blind can be quickly improvised with driftwood and branches. A permanent hunting blind is positioned so that the prevailing winds are at the shooter's back, because ducks decoy into the wind. Portable

Duck Blind shot: For waterside shooting, you can shoot from your regular hunting blind.

46

blinds are also placed, when possible, so that the wind comes from behind.

If the game is to simulate duck hunting the best procedure is to have at least three persons participating—the gunner in the blind and two throwers, one on each side along the shore line. (Since ducks seldom fly into decoys directly overhead and from the rear, it would be unrealistic to throw clays from behind, as straight-away targets.) The throwers should position themselves about thirty or forty yards from the shooting spot and throw the targets so that they present "passing across" shots. For the sake of practice, the gunner may want to shoot singles thrown from both sides. But with doubles, both throwers should be positioned on one side of the blind. In my many years of duck hunting I have never seen ducks cross in front of the blind simultaneously from two directions. Therefore, in doubles, the throwers, standing about ten yards apart, toss out the clays at the same time, or one thrower can hold his throw momentarily so that the second target will fly behind the first, but in the same direction. Being an avid duck hunter, I love this game. However, some of my friends who are non-hunters enjoy this sport as much as I do.

OTHER HAND TRAP GAMES

DOUBLES AND TRIPLES

For experienced gunners, Doubles and Triples present more challenging shooting than singles. Special hand traps make it possible for one thrower to heave out double or triple targets. Two throwers, however, can make the game more interesting. The trap handlers may be positioned on either side of the shooter or they can both throw from the same side. The targets can be heaved out simultaneously or one can held up momentarily so that the second target follows eight or ten yards behind the first. The throwers can move two or three times along the line further away from the shooter, thereby offering targets that fly at different angles. A scoring game is easily devised, and if there is competition, the throwers' positions should be marked so that all participants receive targets of more or less the same degree of difficulty.

WALK-UP SHOTS

Not all hunters are fortunate enough to hunt with dogs, that is, to have their game found, and pointed to, before walking up to flush out the birds from cover. So, they do it the hard way, walking the fields hoping to scare up a pheasant, grouse, or quail.

The game of Walk-up Shots is not only a substantial sport for experienced shooters, it is also a practical way of preparing the gunner for the hunting season. It sharpens the eye and reflexes and, if done regularly, gives the sportsman exercise in the field—an important factor in reducing fatigue and accidents resulting from fatigue.

The shooter and the hand trap man (who carries a shoulder bag of clays so that they don't break in transit) decide on a path or a course to negotiate. The thrower, walking with a loaded hand trap at a convenient distance behind the shooter unexpectedly yells, "bird!", and immediately releases the clay in a direction that presents a feasible target. From a safety point of view the thrower must have had enough practice heaving clays so as not to hit the gunner. An ideal set-up in the Walk-up is to have two throwers following the gunner. All sorts of challenging angles then can be presented to the walking shooter, including doubles. The throwers can signal each other occasionally. For example, displaying a raised arm with two fingers extended would signify doubles.

FLOATERS

All of the preceding games indicate fast targets mostly simulating the quarry in speedy flight. However, as a change-of-pace shot and also as a way of presenting newcomers with easier targets, the "floater" can be of value. A well-practiced thrower is needed to float out slow "teasers" for the experienced shooter as well as tossing up slow moving targets for the neophyte.

4 - Portable Machine Games

Both the hand trap and the portable trap machine throw standard trap and skeet targets, but that's where the similarity ends. The portable machine has many advantages over the hand trap. Obviously, it is not as easily transported as the hand trap that can be placed anywhere in your automobile. When attached to a base, the practice trap takes up most of the room in the trunk of a conventional car, and it is best conveyed in a station-wagon-type vehicle. Once set in place in the field, however, it is far superior to the hand

A group at Yale University's Outdoor Education Center uses a portable trap at the University's Annual Winter Field Day. The portable trap serves in clay target games that cannot be executed on the trap and skeet fields.

trap for use in the informal clay target games. It is lightweight and easily moved from one spot to another; it throws regulation trap and skeet distances and farther; it throws singles and doubles, and some models throw triples. It is simple to operate, sets up quickly and can be held rigidly in place without permanent anchorage. Most models are adjustable without tools, and in some types the angle of flight is designated simply by the position in which the clay target is placed on the throwing arm.

Protect your operator at all times from both the direct discharge of the gun and possible ricochet of the pellets. The illustration shows a trap pit for permanent set-up. Always remove at least the spring and arm when trap is not in use so that children and trespassers will not be injured.

The one aspect in which the portable machine is greatly superior to the hand trap is the consistency of flight of the clay targets. Once the tension of the spring is set for distance and the mechanism adjusted for height, the targets are thrown with a steady flat flight and high speed rotation. Discounting wind influence, the direction, height and speed of the target are always about the same, an obvious advantage over the hand trap when informal clay target games are being played. When instructing new shooters, especially children, the portable trap again is greatly advantageous because it can be positioned for straight-ahead shots. And the anxiety of the new shooter not knowing *exactly* where the clay is going to fly (as is the case when a hand trap is used) is eliminated.

Readers interested in trying one of the *Portable Machine Games* should first study the corresponding section in the previous chapter.

50

UPLAND GAME SHOOT

The shooter, in comparing the practice trap with the hand trap, will quickly realize that some of the informal clay target games conducted with the hand trap cannot be conveniently carried out with the practice or portable trap. For the "upland game shoot," for instance, which consists of four events— Rabbit Run, Quail Shots, Flying Pheasant, and Flying Doves—three traps would be necessary because left, center, and right flying targets are required. However, if three traps were used (one for each direction) the "upland shoot" would be one of the best of the clay target games. The throwing machine is easily adjusted to change the height of the flying targets after the shooters complete each event.

DUCK SHOOTS

The Passing Ducks shoot is another hand-trap game that is not easily adaptable to the portable trap (see Hand-trap Games). Two machines are necessary, and they have to be moved during the exercise because the procedure requires that the distance between gunner and the throwing machines be increased after each round is completed. In this event, however, the trap can be easily adjusted to throw a higher target after each gunner shoots a round at a right and a left target.

DUCKS DECOYING

The use of a practice trap is ideal for the Ducks Decoying game. If the machine is set up on a high cliff, clay bank, or a sand dune, as mentioned previously it can be adjusted to drop the targets at the correct spot in front of the gunner. Also, since the trap's pull cord can be any length, the trap can be placed closer to the edge of the embankment, and the puller can move further back, making the game safer and distracting the shooter less.

HIGH-FLYING DUCKS

Similar to the Ducks Decoying game, this is a perfect game for the stationary practice trap. This event is described further in the preceding chapter.

DUCK BLIND SHOTS

The Duck Blind Shots games is best carried out by use of hand traps, for obvious reasons. It may be inconvenient to carry practice traps to a shoreline duck blind, or to a "make believe" blind, especially if the water edge area is a good distance away from a road. However, if the two traps can be placed in a fairly isolated waterfront area, perhaps in front of a cabin or cottage used for hunting or fishing weekends or vacations, the Duck Blind Shots game is a valuable addition to any outdoor recreation plan.

OTHER PORTABLE MACHINE GAMES

In order to make any "do it yourself" practice trap game more interesting or more difficult for experienced shooters, doubles and triples may be included as a special event or added to the various other games.

WALK-UP SHOTS

The practice trap game of Walk-up Shots differs from its hand-trap counterpart. The walking gunner, instead of being followed by the thrower or throwers, starts from a distance of about twenty yards from the practice trap and then walks toward the trap with his gun in the alert position. The puller may pull the cord to release the arm of the trap as soon as the shooter is standing on the mark, in ready position, or at any time during the walk up to the trap. This game is also called Grouse Walk and it may be played with singles or doubles targets.

In one variation of the Grouse Walk, a number of traps are hidden along both sides of a fence. Two gunners walk along, shoulder to shoulder, one on each side of the fence. The gunner on the right shoots targets appearing on his side only. The gunner on the left takes shots on his side only.

Various other practices and games can be initiated, depending on the ingenuity of the participants. For example, Rabbit Run singles and doubles can be shot while the runner stands on a solid platform, about four feet

52

above the ground. The height supplies a new dimension of shooting down at the targets, just like trying to hit rabbits. The trap can also be secured to a barrel top several feet above ground, thereby adding still another type of shot in height.

5 - Trap Field Novelty Games

The regulation trap field offers a facility for some unusual and exciting shooting. The Rabbit Run, Grouse Walk, and Protection (also called Back-up Trap) are the three games most commonly used as the fun games arranged at the trap field. At the Yale University Shooting Fields we tried a new game that I named Jump Shooting, and it became so popular that we now use it regularly as one of our informal or fun games.

RABBIT RUN

In the Rabbit Run game, the throwing machine is set so that the targets fly as close to the ground as possible. The shooter stands on top and in the center of the trap house, assuming, of course, that the roof is substantially built and will safely hold the gunner. The first participant takes three shots; the other gunners follow in turn. This procedure is followed eight times and each person therefore uses twenty-four shells. The twenty-fifth or extra shell may be used following the first miss or the agreement may be for everyone to shoot four shots the last time on deck.

If the rabbit game is carried out with doubles targets, the gunners can shoot two rounds, that is, four shots at each turn. If this system is followed six times, twenty-four shells will be consumed with the twenty-fifth shot offered as an additional single bird the last time each gunner shoots.

GROUSE WALK

The Grouse Walk or Quail Walk is another contest that quickly separates the men from the boys. This game can be played with one of two shots allowed at singles targets. Or the game could involve doubles. Regardless of the system employed, the shooter loads his gun at Station 3 and walks in a straight line towards the center of the trap house. The puller may release the target immediately upon hearing "ready" from the gunner on Station 3, or he can release the target at any point along the shooter's path between Station 3 and the trap house. At times, the puller will allow the shooter to walk all the way to the trap house before letting out the target. Or he may have the gunner wait for several seconds before the target emerges. Not more than a wait of three to five seconds is fair to the gunner standing up against the trap house. The participant can walk at any rate of speed, but at no time can he stop or use a hesitant gait.

Rabbit Run: If your gun club has traphouses with roofs strong enough to support a shooter's weight, here's a good game to lend variety to your program. Shooter stands atop the house and fires at targets which skim a foot or so above the ground. They appear underfoot and depart at various angles at great speed. The trap throwing angle is depressed and spring tension is increased to pitch targets low to the ground that will reach out forty yards or more from the traphouse.

Grouse Walk. In this game the target is thrown at any time during the shooter's walk. At some clubs, the game is played with doubles being thrown. The club that has its trap field superimposed on the skeet field can add still more variety to the game using all three machines.

PROTECTION

The Protection or Back-up Trap game calls for five teams of two men each to take positions, one team to each station, twenty yards or more from the trap house. The game is the same as regulation American trap, except that two shooters on the same team have a chance to hit the target. Both shoulder their guns in a ready position. When the target is called for, the person on the left shoots first. If he hits the target his teammate does not fire. If he misses the clay, his partner then shoots at it. If the second shooter fires at a target his teammate has hit, or before his partner fires, the target is automatically scored as a miss.

The sequence of shooting is the same as in regulation trap, except that two gunners, instead of one, are standing at each of the five stations. Shooting is done in rotation with the team on Station 1 firing first and the others

"Protection" is a two-man team game for trap. This is an ideal game for husband-wife and father-son combinations, but should only be played by experienced gun-handlers. If your club has a superimposed trap-skeet field, with the No. 8 skeet post coinciding with the No. 3 sixteen yard trap post, it's possible to enjoy "Protection" shooting at skeet targets from trap positions, starting back at the twenty-yard marker or more distant. Throw singles targets only from unannounced houses. While the target source is unknown to the shooters, the fun and laughter are predictable.

following in turn. After each team has fired at five targets from a particular station, all move one position to the right until all teams have fired from the five stations.

JUMP SHOOTING

I call this game Jump Shooting because the flight of the clay targets, rising at fairly close range from the trap house and veering off suddenly away from the shooter in an unexpected direction, is reminiscent of waterfowl bursting from cover when startled by an oncoming duck boat—say in a shallow marsh. The same type of "jump shots" are presented when the hunter, trudging towards a marsh pothole created by the receding tide, "jumps" an unsuspecting duck into the air.

The game plan requires eight stations aligned with the front edge of the trap house, four to the left of the house and four to the right. The two stations closest to the house should be marked about twelve feet from it. The second station on each side is marked six feet from the first, and the other stations are also six feet apart. The first shooter positioned at the first marker on the left side of the trap house (Station 1), calls for the target and shoots at it. After the rest of the squad has done likewise, the procedure is repeated twice more at the station. The same order is followed at the other three positions (Stations 2, 3, and 4) on the left side of the trap house. Then, the squad moves to the right of the house and repeats the same action. By shooting three shots at each of the eight stations, twenty-four shells are expended. The twenty-fifth or extra shell can be used as an extra shot at the station where the first missed target occurs. Or it can be fired as a fourth shot at the last position, Station 8.

6 - Skeet Field Novelty Games

The skeet field is an excellent facility for experimenting with different types of games whose flying targets resemble field shots in hunting. Shooting at double targets at all stations is one of the favorite contests. Another scheme, and variations of it, may be called Pigeon Shoot or Dove Shoot, in which the contestant is presented with a target unexpectedly while walking with gun at the ready position, as in hunting.

DOUBLES ALL STATIONS

In this game the action is just as the name implies. Two targets are released simultaneously, one from the high house and the other from the low house. Each shooter takes his turn at all stations, thereby firing at sixteen targets. The game can end at that point, or the nine shells remaining in the box may be used for "walk-up doubles" from Stations 3, 4, and 5. If such be the case, the gunners, in turn, fire at two sets of doubles at Station 4 and at one set of doubles at Stations 3 and 5. The extra or ninth shell can be shot as a repeat of the first miss.

Obviously, this game is for experienced shooters, whether the entire game is played or just the first series of doubles. In the second or "walk-up" part of the event, the gunner starts walking towards Station 8 with gun lowered in a typical hunting position. The puller releases the birds unexpectedly at any distance the shooter reaches between the beginning station and Station 8. The gunner, while walking, must not stop or hesitate in stride before the clay target is released.

DOVE SHOOT

The following description of a walk-up shoot gives an idea of the type of fast shooting game that can be developed on the skeet field with target opportunities that resemble field shots in hunting. I have named this scheme Dove Shoot, because it presents the shooter with excellent reproductions of the various, fast swinging shots required to bring down a white-wing dove or a mourning dove.

The Dove Shoot is entirely a walking game. The stations are set up the same as in Doubles All Stations. Each station, except No. 7, is used as a starting point from which the gunners, in turn, walk towards Station 8. The puller may release the target anytime during the gunner's advance toward Station 8. For obvious safety reasons, Station 7 is eliminated as a starting area. Instead, a position between Stations 6 and 7 is used; it is called Station 7B as a reminder against using Station 7. The scheme is as follows:

1. Each gunner shoots at a high house single from all stations (1 through 7B).
2. In reverse order of stations (7B through 1) the squad members fire at a low house single from each station.
3. Next, each person shoots at a single at Stations 2 through 6. In this series however, the target may emerge from the high house or the low house at the discretion of the puller.
4. Doubles are shot at Stations 3, 4, and 5.

HANDICAP SKEET

The novelty Handicap Skeet game consists simply of having an unusually good shooter stand two or three yards behind the regular stations when shooting with gunners of lesser ability. Caution must be exercised here. The other members of the squad must also move back the same distance while the handicap shooter is ready to fire.

7 - Special Facility Shoots

Several of the most unique of the novel clay target games require special facilities and management by a gun club, shooting preserve, or independent group of shooters. Many gun clubs have constructed such specialized installations on a permanent basis.

CRAZY QUAIL

Crazy Quail, developed in Texas, is one of the most exciting of clay target games. Targets, emerging from a pit, are thrown in a 360 degree circle from a single trap, with safe distances of 300 yards in the direction of the firing. The practice trap is welded onto a vertical shaft. At the bottom of the pit, attached to the shaft, is a seat for the puller or target releaser; the seat swings around the shaft in a complete circle. The gunners usually stand ready to shoot at a sixteen yard marker, but longer distances (up to twenty-seven yards) may be used. The puller may release the target to fly in any direction, including directly at the shooter. And the target may be withheld for up to ten seconds after the shooter yells "Pull." The gunner, for obvious reasons of safety, is not allowed to shoot at the target once it has passed him. Some installations include a wooden frame to prevent the shooter from swinging too far.

The seven-foot-square pit is usually about six feet deep. Pit sides may be corrugated aluminum or galvanized steel. A mound of dirt may be placed in front of the pit as an added safety for the target releaser. The mound can be made to look natural by planting local shrubs around it. Some clubs set up full-sized, naturally painted, silhouettes of dogs at point at each end of the mound.

Drainage in the pit can be a problem. In an area of poor drainage, the trap can be situated at ground level and a higher protective mound built up around it. In a permanent arrangement, a drainage pipe can be installed in the bottom of the pit.

Although most clubs build their own Crazy Quail setup, there is a manufacturer that sells the complete unit. Pit plans and information concerning

Crazy Quail set-up. Note seat for trap handler. The trap can be revolved to throw targets in any direction.

Gunner on station waiting for Crazy Quail target to fly from pit.

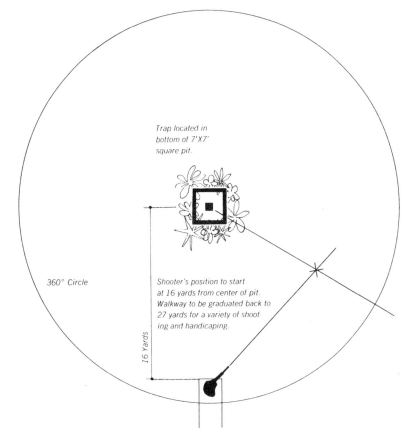

Trap located in
bottom of 7'X7'
square pit.

360° Circle

Shooter's position to start
at 16 yards from center of pit.
Walkway to be graduated back to
27 yards for a variety of shooting and handicaping.

16 Yards

The Crazy Quail layout.

manufacturers of commercial units are available from the National Shooting
Sports Foundation, 1075 Post Road, Riverside, Conn. 06878.

Crazy Quail is a fun game, and shooters may make up their own rules for
competition. The facility is also adaptable for teaching beginners to shoot.
The trap can be held at a constant angle and the spring tension can be eased
for a slower target. Also, the neophyte can move in closer to the pit.

DUCK TOWER SHOOT

This is another of the clay-target games that is especially attractive to
hunters. The tower can be of any convenient height depending upon the
site. The house on top of the trap can be just large enough to hold a mechanical trap, or it can be big enough to protect the person who is working
a hand-loading machine. When using a trap that throws in a single direction,

the shooters can change stations in order to be presented with targets at different angles.

An attractive permanent layout can be created by erecting three to five stations, appropriately separated and arranged in a semi-circle so that they face a tower, in which is housed a mechanical throwing machine similar to one used in trap shooting. The stations can be built to resemble actual duck hunting blinds. Gunners may change blinds after every five shots. And they can make up their own shooting rules.

Duck Tower. The shooters can also be positioned in front of the tower to shoot at targets flying directly overhead.

RIVERSIDE SKEET

This is a clay-target competition developed in 1948 by shooters at the Riverside Yacht Club, Riverside, Connecticut. The scheme includes five stations arranged to resemble a standard trap-shooting facility. The stations are wooden platforms four feet square and about six inches above ground. A hand loading machine (manual trap), anchored in a concrete block, is safely located at each end of the line. The traps are angled so that when doubles are thrown the targets cross at about twenty-five yards.

The shooter at Station 1 gets a left-hand single, then a right-hand single. His third shot is a single at the option of the releasers. (A signal system is

Riverside Skeet is a clay target game developed in 1948 by shooters at the Riverside Yacht Club, Riverside, Conn. It is known in southern Connecticut as that "Blankety Blank Riverside Skeet."

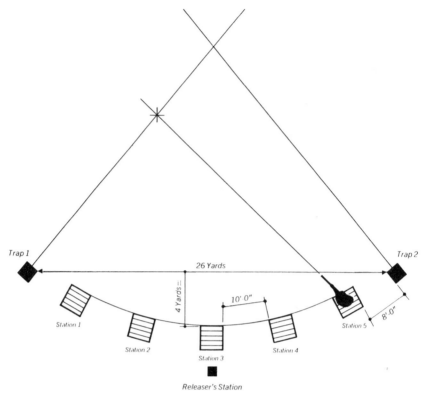

The Riverside Skeet field layout.

used by the two releasers.) After the third shot, the gunner at Station 2 takes his turn, and so on until all five gunners have fired three rounds. Station 1 then fires doubles. After all stations have fired a double, all shooters rotate, in the same manner as in standard trap shooting. Shooters can work out many variations of the game, and trap angles can be varied to make shooting more difficult.

MINI-TRAP

The Mini-Trap, a qualification or awards course for .410 shotguns, was introduced by the National Rifle Associaton. Although Mini-Trap uses standard clay targets, the shooting field is half the size of a regulation trap field. The field is set up in a clearing about 210 yards long and 75 yards wide. The stations are located twenty-five feet from the front edge of the trap house. The distance between stations is five feet on centers. (Field layout plans and construction outlines for the Mini-Trap facility are treated in Chapter 7.)

In shooting for NRA qualification ratings, the trap must be adjusted to heave the target approximately thirty-five yards. And the trap should be mounted so that it inclines at an angle of thirty to thirty-five degrees, with the front higher than the back.

Any .410 shotgun may be used. Also, any break-open 12-, 16- or 20-gauge gun may be used if it is equipped with a .410 gauge chamber adapter. Shooters must use regular commercial .410 gauge, 2½ inch shotshell containing not more than ½ ounce of shot and not heavier than No. 7½. A round consists of ten targets. The gunner fires at two targets from each of five stations. Of course, all the safety precautions used in regular trap shooting should be observed.

Mini-Trap has several advantages over regulation trap. The .410 shotgun is light and the recoil is minimal compared to that of regulation trap and skeet guns. The targets are slower and more easily hit, thereby encouraging the neophyte; a very important factor wih new shooters. And .410 shells cost less than 12-gauge ammo.

Shooters or organizations interested in initiating a program of qualifications and awards should write to the offices of the NRA.

QUAIL WALK

Another clay target game that closely simulates field shooting is the multiple-trap Quail Walk. No limit is set on the number of traps employed. As few as four or as many as a dozen traps may be used. The traps are laid out along a winding path, where they are hidden behind shrubs, rocks, embankments, etc. Their trip cords are also camouflaged. The puller follows a few yards behing the gunner and pulls the cords that release the traps. If one shooter walks the path he shoots at targets emerging from either side of the path. If two gunners negotiate the course, one takes the right targets and the other, the left. After each round, the angle of the flying clays can be easily changed by turning the portable traps slightly. For safety, common sense dictates that the throwing machines are positioned so that the clay birds fly out in directions that do not jeopardize the gunner. And it takes a bit of experimenting when setting the release spring of the trap. The tension should be lowered to more clearly resemble the flight speed of quail, especially if the course site is a wooded area or in heavy, high brush.

GROUSE WALK

The Grouse Walk is a shooting exercise that closely resembles the Quail Walk. But instead of the throwing machines being set along a winding path they are hidden on both sides of a railing fence or a hedgerow. Two gunners, shoulder to shoulder, walk along the fence, one at each side. The shooter on the right fires at the targets emerging on his side, and his companion on the left shoots only at clays emerging on his side. The long release cord to each trap can be set through eye-hooks under the top rail of the fence. The puller releases the concealed machine by pulling the ring attached to the end of the cord.

SPECIAL EVENTS

The Turkey Shoot has been a shotgun game ever since Americans started using shotguns. It is usually held in the fall around the Thanksgiving holiday. The program may consist of several of the shooting games, including or combining regulation trap and skeet with the novelty clay target games. Today, oven-ready frozen turkeys or hams are awarded as prizes. A fee is charged either to enter individual events, or to participate in all segments of the program.

A Turkey Shoot.

The multiple event program is offered by gun clubs whose membership is composed exclusively of experienced shooters. Other organizations, however, may use a single shotgun event with other activities such as archery and .22 rifle target shooting.

An excellent one-event game for a fund raising at a church outing, for example, is called Lucky Target. A steel plate with a three-inch hole cut out of its center is positioned at a distance of twenty or twenty-five yards from the shooter. A white piece of paper is taped over the hole on the back side of the plate. The number of pellets that go through the paper are counted and a record of each shooter's score is recorded. The highest number of pellet holes wins the turkey. In case of a tie, the participants have a shoot-off. The gun used in this event is a .410 gauge. The cost of entering the shoot is set by the outing committee, and is usually something like fifty cents or a dollar a try. In this type of public event where many participants have never before fired a shotgun, extreme caution must be exercised by the supervisors running the contest. They must be experienced shooters, thoroughly familiar with the shotgun. The gun must be loaded and handed to the shooter with safety on. The overseer must also stand by the shooter and release the safety *after* the participant shoulders the gun. A table should be placed immediately ahead of the shooter's station. The gun, when not in actual use, should recline with action open on the table. As an added precaution to prevent the neophyte from swinging inadvertently away from the

66

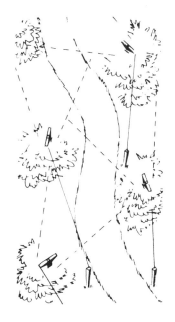

This is a multiple-trap walk. As few as four or as many as a dozen or more traps may be used. The traps can be adjusted for various angles. The targets are released as the shooter walks along the path. If one shooter participates he can shoot at any and all targets. If two shooters travel the course, one takes the right targets and the other, the left.

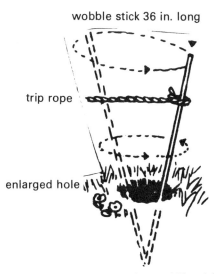

wobble stick 36 in. long

trip rope

enlarged hole

Tripping device. Shown is a wobble stick which lets the shooter release the trap from a distance without use of hands. This is used primarily when the shooter wants to shoot alone. The shooter trips the trap by leaning against the stick.

direction of the steel plate, two pieces of plywood, two or three feet square can be framed on the table. All shooting then takes place between the plywood baffles, within an area about three feet wide.

There are other ways of playing the Lucky Target games. A card board

67

or stiff paper, about three feet square, is tacked to a frame. Marked on the paper is a circle about a foot-and-a-half in diameter. The circle is also marked like a thinly sliced pie but in thinner slices. Each contestant pays a fee to write his or her name in one of the slices. When all the slices are signed, the coordinator of the event, using a 12-gauge shotgun, shoots at the diagram from a distance of about thirty yards. The slice that receives the most pellets wins the turkey.

In another version of the same event, each contestant draws a circle, on any part of the card board, using a fifty-cent piece or a beer coaster as a form. The participant signs his name in the circle. The circle getting the greatest number of pellets wins the prize.

One of the most popular of Lucky Target methods involves skeet shooting. It is called the *Lewis Class System* because, I suppose, it was invented by a Mr. Lewis. The cost of the turkeys (or other prizes) is taken into consideration, and the number of winners is determined by the amount of profit the club expects to make. The system works this way: the gunners' scores are posted in order of the number of targets hit in one round of skeet. A turkey is presented to the shooter with the highest posted score. Ties can be decided by a flip of a coin. But the remaining turkeys reserved for the event go to lucky shooters, not to the best shooters. It might be decided, for instance, that if thirty shooters are expected to take part, shooters scoring in the tenth, twentieth, or thirtieth places will receive a prize.

Two other novel shooting games that are often employed in turkey shoots, sometimes as part of the whole program, sometimes as individual events with specific prizes, are Handicap Trap and Mo-Skeet. The trap game involves five shots, one shot from the regular sixteen-yard station and the other four from eighteen, twenty, twenty-two, and twenty-four yards.

Mo-Skeet involves a mini-machine and mini-clay targets. The gun used is a smooth bore .22 rifle and the ammunition is a .22 rim fire cartridge loaded with No. 11 shot. The gunner stands directly behind the trap. Usually, the required number of targets for the competition is five. However, the rules can be varied depending on the particular situation. For example, the elevation or the angle of the flying targets can be changed after every two or three shots by each shooter. Or the gunner's position may be changed to right or left of the trap.

PART II
MASTERING THE BASICS

8 - Human Elements

Four principal factors have a direct bearing on a person's shooting ability, whether that person is a neophyte, a world champion, or somewhere in between. These four factors are psychology, physiology, kinesiology, and *physical fitness*. Each has a prime influence on a shooter's scores. The great majority of shooters are unaware of these controlling factors, but there is no doubt that any shooter who is subject to a particular weakness associated with these four human elements can improve his shooting considerably.

PSYCHOLOGY IN CLAY TARGET SHOOTING

Every knowledgeable coach, regardless of his sport, recognizes the importance of the psychological factor in individual and team performance. Individual team members are influenced to some degree by the psychological responses of the team, and the team as a whole is influenced by the psychological impact of each individual. As shooters, coaches, and administrators should be aware, the psychological factor also plays a role in numerous aspects of clay target shooting, whether the sport is indulged in competitively or for recreation only. For one thing, the individual's own psychology—his response, for instance, to an improving or worsening score—can affect his shooting ability. Looked at from another perspective, the very act of shooting can affect the individual's mental health, providing a socially acceptable means of releasing pent-up tensions. In yet another aspect, the attitudes and behavior of both coach and student can have an important bearing on the success or failure of efforts to teach gunning and clay-target shooting (a subject that is discussed more fully elsewhere in this book).

One way in which the behavior of many trap and skeet shooters allow their own behavior to have a detrimental effect on their shooting skill is by indulging in practices that are nothing more than superstitions. Take, for example, the shooter who, in reloading his hulls, shies away from reloading shells that have missed a target. Such superstition will certainly have an adverse effect on his shooting, because he is thinking negatively. Subconsciously, he is thinking about throwing away hulls rather than hitting targets.

Again superstitiously, some trapshooters, while waiting their turn to shoot, take great care to place the shell in the chamber in such a way that the headstamping can be read. Psychologically, this type of behavior is detrimental to total concentration, because somewhere in the recesses of his mind the shooter will be wondering: "Did I or didn't I insert the shell correctly?"

How about the shooter who blows the smoke out of his gun barrel after every shot? The feeling among many of these "smoke blowers" is that if they don't blow into the barrel they increase their chances of missing the next shot, the theory being that some of the energy of the shot charge is lost if it has to push the smoke out of the barrel before flying out at the target. Again, to be preoccupied with such irrelevances while on station can be more of a detriment psychologically than a benefit.

Another common sight at shooting fields is the gunner who refuses to be lead off man in his squad. Does he believe that his performance will be improved if he observes the targets beforehand, or does he fear that a miss will be more noticeable if he is the first person to fire at a target at each station? Either way, his attitude is self defeating.

Now consider the man on station who accidentally drops a shell on the ground and kicks it aside rather than picking it up and placing it in the gun chamber. *His* action has nothing to do either with psychology or superstition; it is good, common sense. Bending over sends blood rushing to the head; straightening up quickly may affect equilibrium. Also, some persons' eyes do not focus quickly enough when shifting from looking for the dropped shell close by and then searching for the distant flying target. Such behavior has a sound physiological basis.

Many other instances of behavior detrimental to accurate shooting are seen on the shooting fields, but I will limit myself here to adding the following examples associated with concentration, the most important of all the psychological influences in shooting clay targets.

In trap and skeet shooting, concentration means to shut out all distractions and focus undivided attention on the target. It is agreed among clay target enthusiasts that given two gunners of equal physical ability on the shooting stations, the one with the greater powers of concentration will end up with the better score. But how the individual gunners prepare themselves for this important concentration is an interesting psychological phenomenon.

One of my good friends, who is an extremely capable skeet shooter, told me confidentially that each night, several days before a competitive shoot, he puts out the lights in his room and, in total darkness and with no distractions, shoulders his gun and swings at, and hits, every target he pictures in his mind. He performs this action on each target exactly as it flies in a round of skeet. And he continues his performance for the number of rounds to be shot in the match or tournament. He believes that by doing this he "psyches" himself gradually to the point where total concentration will become automatic when he reaches the firing station. I believe that the exercise is a good one for arm endurance and the elimination of fatigue during long shoots. As for this business of "psyching up," I think that more harm than good would be done psychologically if for some reason he had to forego this ritual, especially if he were intending to do it the night before the shoot and could not. On the other hand, perhaps exercise of the mind in the dark should not be taken too lightly, because it is practiced by one of the world's best International Skeet shooters, Brad Simmons, captain of Yale University's Trap and Skeet Team and a member of the U.S. Olympic team.

Then there are the competitors who hope for total concentration on the field by trying desperately not to think about the shooting until the last possible moment. In the club house they try hard by indulging in much conversation and coffee drinking. There are other gunners who will "spectate" a round of trap or skeet before their squad is scheduled to shoot, carefully following each flying target as if they themselves were going to shoot at it. Many types and variations of these examples are indulged in generally by shot-gunners. It has been my observation that such "psychological idiosyncrasies" add nothing to concentration on targets when shooting. Instead, I believe they contribute to mental duress that may in a long tournament cause fatigue and hence missed targets.

Many theories have been offered concerning specific procedures of concentration in shooting. Personally, I believe that concentration on flying targets immediately before and during shooting is nothing more than an acquired discipline or ability of the mind to cut off or control all distractions the moment the shooter steps onto the skeet station or when he shoulders his gun in trapshooting.

But perhaps a more definitive comment on the psychology of trap and skeet shooting is that offered by Frank DeGrado, who coaches the shooting team at Triton College in Illinois, where he is a Professor of Psychology. Recently I asked him to share his thoughts. on the subject. He graciously complied. The following paragraphs were written by him.

A PSYCHOLOGICAL VIEW OF SHOOTING SPORTS

People, regardless of occupation, place of residence, or education, enjoy shooting. One reason may be that the activity is so far removed from the complexities of everyday life that it possesses a therapeutic quality. I have often heard people say that the sport is a very effective means of unwinding from daily pressures. There is a sense of satisfaction in having control over one's body and its movements, as well as stimulation from the shooting environment and the sense of accomplishment that comes from shooting correctly. There is also a special type of sensation produced by the coordination of brain, body, eye, and gun, similar to that of a dancer mastering an intricate step.

Although many people are dedicated to good shooting, some find shooting an escape. This may be especially true for the professional person with heavy responsibilities and pressures. Sometimes the need to escape may be an effort to free oneself from an unrewarding situation or relationship.

The handicapped are also finding shooting to be a rewarding sport. Participants range from ten- or eleven-year-old children with muscular dystrophy to senior citizens with crippling arthritic conditions. Through the use of special equipment which adapts to a person's handicap, many disabled individuals now are capable of enjoying shooting and even becoming marksmen. For these people shooting provides a means of improving their muscle control as well as enhancing their self image.

The self image is, of course, much more complex than the name suggests. It is by no means free of inconsistencies and fragmentations. For our purposes, however, we may simply think of it as a unified pattern of feelings and behavior. A person becomes as he imagines himself: "As a man thinketh in his heart, so he is."

Shooting provides the handicapped individual with the opportunity to conquer himself and his adversity. It enables him to progress in an activity that is used by his non-handicapped peers. It may be hard work, but his self-concept grows. He has confronted his problem, made a decision, and acted upon it. He has conquered adversity and is no longer handicapped. His self-concept is improved.

The opportunity for individual performance is another source of satisfaction to be derived from the shooting sports. Men and women practice and perform not to become champions but to satisfy themselves. Each person is responsible for standards of skill and accuracy, exclusive of other participants. On the range or in the field, each person develops his own style and succeeds or fails on his own merit.

The many social activities associated with shooting sports promote a sense of belonging, a sense of relatedness, and a sense of solidarity with others. While the specific activity—banquet, dance, picnic, conversation—may vary, the similarity of interests and behaviors offers those involved the pleasures of shared experience.

A formidable task confronts our society. That of maintaining the mental health of its citizens. With all the pressures and tensions of our modern-day world we must find socially acceptable ways to establish and maintain mentally healthy individuals. Recreational shooting is one of many activities that can assist us in achieving this end.

Frustration and boredom, which are so often products of our highly complex society, can be closely linked to the urge to express aggression. If repressed without a suitable outlet the individual's mental health can be endangered. For many people sports shooting can provide the proper balance between the need to express aggression and society's need to confine aggression to acceptable channels.

Nor is this problem confined to the adult population. Growing numbers of children and adolescents are also afflicted with ulcers and nervous tension. It is important that such youths be offered opportunities for the kind of challenge, excitement, and relaxation that are an integral part of the shooting sports. No person young or old need resort to tranquilizers or sedatives to cope with mental stress when recreational activities such as sports shooting are available.

As one studies the relationship of present day pressures to the emotional health of our citizens, one is painfully impressed by the variety of artificial means being used to reduce those pressures. But was it always this way? No! Early Americans participated in numerous physical activities, which were not only necessary for survival but which enabled them to express themselves physically, helping thereby to reduce psychological pressures. But modern man has no such luxury. He is frequently threatened with verbal attacks, speeding autos, insults, and the threat of losing his job. Yet seldom can he deal with these pressures directly. Society demands that he sit quietly and respond maturely, never expressing the churning within. When this difficult state of psychological tension is internalized, it often results in such things as ulcers, heart attacks, and colitis.

How does all this relate to shooting sports? Easily. Among the various sports that can be used as a pressure release, shooting often seems to furnish the right combination of self-expression, individuality, danger, and accomplishment to help modern man bring his psychological being back into balance. The shooting community provides the opportunity for social interactions freed from work pressures and the sense of fellowship that can come from belonging to a group of people who share one's interests. In these ways shooting can often help counterbalance the psychologically upsetting aspects of everyday life.

9 - Physiology

FATIGUE FACTOR

The physiological element that most generally influences the shooting accuracy of experienced trap and skeet competitors is the *fatigue factor*. I am not referring to total exhaustion or the type of fatigue that a shooter may experience after a night of carousing, but to the more subtle but not less important element of hidden fatigue, the kind that is hardly noticeable and that is often ignored by the great majority of shooters, especially the veterans.

Fatigue may creep up on the gunner in the course of shooting in one or more of the following forms: *muscular, mental, ocular, acoustical, thermal,* and *nutritive,* all of which are capable of draining some of the energy that is required for "top-form" shooting.

MUSCULAR FATIGUE

The most common and most pronounced muscular fatigue, the kind that affects the whole body, is suffered by those who force themselves into grandiose squatting, leaning, and leg-spreading positions while on station. Sapping of energy by such muscular strain accumulates slowly, sapping the shooter's energy until, as the shooting progresses into another round, his scores begin to drop.

When any part of the muscular body tires, it affects the responses of the entire system, including eyesight, which has to be keen at all times for good shooting. Body reflexes and eyesight may be only slightly affected by loss of energy through muscle strain, but the effect may still cause targets to be missed and consequently make the difference between a good score and an excellent one, or winning or not winning a championship.

A strained stance is easily corrected. The gunner simply assumes the upright relaxed position (see the beginning of Chapter 3). The correct position will feel awkward at first, and the shooter's scores will suffer, but once the stance is developed, his scores will be higher than they were originally.

Another common, creeping malady not recognized by many shooters is arm weariness. During shoots, when the gunner is not actually shooting, the gun should be held or rested in such a way that its weight is not borne entirely by the arms. On station, pointing the gun for too long before calling for the target is a common cause of fatigue, especially among new shooters. But some veterans, who believe that pointing the gun and staring down the barrel helps their concentration, are also victims.

Any serious shotgun enthusiast who tries to improve his shooting should exercise his arms daily or at least three times a week. Ten minutes of arm and upper body drills will have a positive effect on the arms and shoulders. During actual shooting, the benefits of such exercise will go a long way towards eliminating arm fatigue. The exercise should not be strenuous. The objective is to develop endurance and not necessarily strength. All that is needed for lifting is an object about the weight of a box of shells. The *kinesiology* section contains diagrams identifying the muscles involved and the suggested home or gymnasium exercises to strengthen them.

MENTAL FATIGUE

Some shooters can combat mental fatigue better than others. Of course, the degree of mental fatigue depends upon the individual's personality. Mental stress can affect scores, especially when participating in tournaments away from the shooter's home grounds, when he has to think about motel accommodations, pre-registration, timing for practice sessions, and so forth. The common sense approach to alleviating mental fatigue in such circumstances is to make all arrangements well in advance and not wait until the last moment. Another type of mental fatigue may be brought on by psychological responses (see Chapter 8).

OCULAR CONSIDERATIONS

Tired eyes and good shooting are simply not compatible. A shooter's eyes may be strained or irritated to a point that will subtly affect his shooting ability without the shooter himself being aware of it. If reaching the shooting grounds requires a drive of several hours, a short nap will help rest tired eyes. Sitting in a club house full of cigarette, cigar, or pipe smoke will not only irritate eyes but will also raise the blood pressure of non-smokers and harm their shooting.

Something as obvious as the need for tinted glasses, as a protection from bright sunlight, should not have to be mentioned, yet I constantly see shooters who disregard this imperative. Not only does direct sunlight produce eye strain by constant squinting, but the targets themselves cannot be seen as well. Exposure to glare accelerates body fatigue and contributes to headaches. On an average day our eyes use up about twenty-five percent of our body energy, and when pushed—as in trap and skeet—they draw even more body fuel. Shooters, who believe that watching several rounds of targets

Squatters, leaners, and leg spreaders not only harm their shooting because they invariably rise or restrict swing as they follow the target, but the fatigue factor slowly creeps in to effect their accuracy adversely.

Left elbow too low, right elbow too high, and right foot completely out of position.

If this shooter raised the right elbow it would bring the butt of the stock into a better position in the hollow of her shoulder.

Classic example of a poor shooting posture in International Skeet that is harmful to the gunner's proficiency. Note that the shooter, in a squatting position, raises his body upright as he shoots. His face comes off the stock and his right heel leaves the ground. He must compensate for the vertical rise of his gun besides swinging arms and waist laterally to keep up with the flight of the target.

Leaners also have a tendency to straighten up as they pull the trigger, influencing the possibility of shooting over their target.

Occasionally, by sheer determination and much practice, a shooter, such as Dan Tenney of the Yale National Championship team, will overcome bad arm and leg form to become an excellent shooter. The question remains, however: Would he be a *great* shooter if he used a correct shooting posture?

shot by others will help their concentration are making a mistake. It will only produce eye fatigue, especially on bright days. Close watching should not be done immediately before a gunner expects to shoot because his eyes will not recoup in time for his own shooting.

Excessive reading immediately before going out to the trap or skeet field may be a hindrance to some shooters. During intercollegiate competitions I often see students sitting in their cars deeply engrossed in their books. Perhaps they are feeling pressured to get classroom assignments done. But it stands to reason that eyes that have been focused for an hour at small print about twelve inches away are going to require some time to focus at their best at distant flying targets. Young eyes generally adjust quite quickly, but I believe it would help the shooter if he ended his book reading at least a half hour before the shooting.

Are eye drops useful in soothing or removing irritation? The drops may feel good, but such medication may hinder the focusing of the eyes. Serious tournament competitors who use eye drops would do well to consult an oculist concerning this question.

ACOUSTICAL CONSIDERATIONS

The human ear's reaction or objection to too much noise is not outwardly apparent. However, an abused inner ear may well make its objections felt, causing gun swing hesitancy, flinching, and other subtle faults that are not easily detectable. None of these imperfections may be permanent, but they may occur frequently enough to be reflected in the shooter's scores.

Of course, everyone but a fool wears ear protectors while shooting. But many gunners take off their ear protectors the moment they finish shooting and do not use them again until they are back on the shooting field. It is not uncommon to see a group of participants sitting on a bench close to the firing stations, either watching the other shooters or waiting to shoot. Not one in the squad will have his ear device in place. Ignoring gun blast in such situations, especially in day-long tournaments, can be harmful to the ears, not only by causing immediate miscues in shooting, but also by contributing to the gradual onset of permanent ear damage. Prevention, of course, is simple; wear ear protective devices at all times when you are close enough to gun blast to feel the slightest discomfort.

CLIMATIC THERMAL DISCOMFORT

Hot weather fatigue, that is, loss of energy through overheating, is a summertime hazard caused by excessive loss of water due to perspiration; the

Winter shooting can be great fun, even in a snowstorm, provided the shooters wear proper clothing.

condition lowers general physical efficiency, leads to fatigue and increases chances of missing targets. It can be a serious handicap to trap and skeet shooters, especially for those traveling to a tournament where the climate is distinctly warmer than the one from which they came. Precautions are simple, but necessary. Wear a light-weight hat that has a peak to shade the eyes and that allows ventilation through the sides. A wide-brim straw hat is excellent; don't wear a felt cowboy hat, no matter how dashing it makes you look. Keep eyes cool by wearing sun glasses. Clothing, of course, should be light. Padded-shoulder shooting shirts are good to wear, but if you are traveling from a northern climate in winter to a tournament in, say, Georgia or Texas, wear a shirt that has long sleeves; a sunburn at the bend in your arms will knock your scores down in a hurry. Do not wear tennis or basketball shoes; they offer little protection from the absorbed heat in concrete or asphalt walks and shooting stations. Drink plenty of cooling liquids; water is best. Avoid drinking iced-tea or coffee for a reasonable time before you're scheduled to shoot (reasons why are given later in this chapter, in the section on nutrition). If possible, try to arrive at least a day ahead of the shoot so that your body may have some time to orient to the sudden change in temperature and degree of sunlight. And above all, do not sun bathe until you are completely finished shooting in the tournament. During periods when you are not actually shooting, sit in the shade, and rest at every opportunity.

GENERAL PHYSICAL CONDITION

Naturally, in a squad of shooters of equal ability, those who are physically fit will outscore those who are not. To be in good physical condition for shooting one does not necessarily have to go to a gymnasium or jog so many miles, or swim so many laps in a pool, or lift weights. Do the simple exercises prescribed in the kinesiology section to prevent muscle fatigue of the arms. Walk whenever possible. I do not mean you have to go long distances; a comfortably vigorous walk daily during your lunch hour can be just as beneficial. Walk to different sandwich shops. Do some window shopping. Walk, stop, stand and continue again. This is exactly the kind of activity you encounter on the trap and skeet fields, from the moment you enter the club house to wait to be registered for a squad until you leave the last shooting station—activity that might be called "disruptive endurance."

NUTRITION

Improper eating or drinking, before and during a period of clay target competition, may affect a shooter's scores. Improper nutritional intake may contribute to—or be totally responsible for—tiredness, lack of endurance, irritability, or discomfort on the shooting field. It may also affect a person's ability to handle the stress which inevitably accompanies serious, competitive shooting.

The shooter who participates in a day-long competition and believes that nutritional factors are a lot of nonsense should be aware that more energy is expended by a gunner in a day of tournament shooting than by an athlete who participates in an hour of football, basketball, track or swimming.

Nutritional factors begin playing a role in our lives from the moment we are conceived. The type and amount of food one consumes affects one's ultimate size, strength and stamina. Nutritional research has produced much information concerning the nutrient needs of people of different ages and conditions. For example, the published guidelines, Recommended Daily Dietary Allowances, have been set up by the Food and Nutrition Board, National Academy of Science, National Research Council for planning dietary considerations under different situations. However, we are not concerned here with the science of nutrition as a whole, but simply with what and when to eat and drink before and during a shooting event to prevent the temporary or momentary afflictions that may affect shooting.

Instead of indulging in theories and technicalities about how poor eating habits, over a period of time, may affect the long-run potential of anyone participating in competitive sports, let's consider a typical day of shooting. Aside from cautioning my Yale Trap and Skeet members to drink beer modestly (if they have to drink at all) the night before a match or tournament, and to get at least eight hours of sleep, I suggest the following dietary regimen:

BREAKFAST

This is an especially important meal if the shooting schedule calls for morning participation; don't skip it. Studies indicate to omit breakfast is to invite fatigue and laxness late in the morning. For an active person to be mentally and physically alert, about one-third of the day's food should be taken at breakfast. Coffee and toast or a sugared muffin do not provide a satisfactory breakfast. Fried eggs and bacon are not recommended if morning shooting is scheduled, because when fat enters the intestinal tract it causes the release of a hormone, enterogastrone, which slows down the stomach's evacuation time. As a result, a visit to the club house john may become necessary late in the morning, when the shooter is in the midst of a round of shooting. However, normal young persons can tolerate fat to a greater extent than older people. Moderate amounts of foods, properly fried, can be consumed without interfering with the shooter's scheduled bowel movements. Perhaps the best advice on this issue is for the individual to recognize the fact that the fatty foods at breakfast *may* have some effect on physical well being during morning shooting, and to experiment accordingly.

The breakfast menu recommended by investigators studying these issues is: a citrus fruit or juice, cereal and/or toast and a milk drink.

SNACKS

Snacks, taken between shooting rounds can be an asset, if properly chosen. Try to stay away from carbonated beverages, sugars, candy, and especially tea and coffee. Milk, fruit, crackers or plain pastries are best. Milk, milk-shakes, other milk drinks, and cheese are especially good when extra energy is needed.

LUNCH

It is just plain common sense not to overload your stomach at lunch if shooting is scheduled for early afternoon, but it is surprising how many shooters under the circumstances will eat two hamburgers and drink two cups of coffee or coke when one hamburger and a glass of milk will overcome sluggishness.

DINNER

If the tournament participant must shoot in early evening, at a time beyond his usual dinner hour, he should partake of something light, such as a peanut butter sandwich and a glass of milk. A full dinner just before shooting is obviously unwise.

SUMMARY

There is no way that a certain rigid diet can be prescribed for everyone participating in extended clay-target events. Each person's physiological characteristics must be considered. However, all of the preceding information will be of value if it does nothing more than alert the gunner to the fact that nutritional demands are greater than expected when participating in prolonged matches and tournaments. The shooter should analyze his own reactions to types of food and amounts consumed under given circumstances.

BEVERAGES

MILK

Experts in nutrition state that milk is one of the most nearly "perfect" foods, and if not taken for a period of time, the nutrients calcium, phosphorus, and riboflavin may be inadequate. Science has not produced any basis for eliminating milk from the athlete's diet. Actually, it is an excellent source of protein.

Milk will not produce dryness and discomfort in the mouth (cotton mouth) experienced by some shooters. Studies indicate that saliva flow and the condition of the saliva are related to the amount of perspiration and reduction of body water content. When it is time for a shooter to appear on the field, his saliva flow may be influenced by his emotional state. Another common fallacy is that if milk is consumed before shooting time it will cause "curdling," resulting in sour stomach. When milk combines with stomach acids, the curdling that results is a natural process of digestion and does not result in stomach disturbance. On the contrary, milk may combat excess stomach acidity by neutralizing the acids. As stated previously, milk, milkshakes, and cheese are among the best of snacking foods when the demand for extra energy arises.

COFFEE

Tea is often thought to be preferable to coffee by persons participating in gunning and other athletic events. However, both coffee and tea contain caffeine, a temporary stimulant. A cup of coffee contains about 0.1 to 0.15 grams of caffeine. A cup of strong tea has about 0.1 gram of caffeine. Both beverages, if the gunner is addicted to them, should be taken in moderation. Tea can be taken very light by removing the tea bag sooner. But neither of these beverages lessens fatigue for any length of time. Coffee is of no benefit to the shooter; on the contrary, it may be detrimental. A strong cup of coffee tends to increase urine flow and stimulates oxygen consumption. The caffeine that it harbors not only has negligible energy value, but strongly stimulates the cardiac muscles, thereby increasing force of contraction, heart rate, and cardiac output. It causes nervousness rather than alertness in many shooters; it makes blood pressure go up, speeds up breathing, and forces the adrenal glands to pour out the hormones that make the nervous system work harder. Some gunners who are heavy coffee drinkers do not realize that this beverage is injurious to their shooting. Others are well aware of it, but cannot refuse coffee before and in between trap or skeet rounds, because they are addicted to it just as badly as a habitual cigarette smoker is to smoking.

CARBONATED AND OTHER SWEETENED BEVERAGES

These drinks mostly contribute calories and fluids. Some of them, such as the cola drinks, contain caffeine in varying amounts, and therefore are considered stimulants, along with tea and coffee. If not intended to replace other liquid foods, particularly milk, carbonated beverages may be used in moderation.

ALCOHOLIC DRINKS

Any form of alcohol is a depressant of the human central nervous system, and even small amounts affect the finer movements of the body's coordination. Coordination is affected to a greater extent when larger amounts are consumed. Anyone having more than a drink or two at dinner, the night before a shoot is making a mistake. Any person drinking alcohol in any form during a shoot should be immediately barred from competition and ordered to leave the premises.

WATER REQUIREMENTS

Just about every operation or motion of the body needs water. Digestion and proper utilization of foods cannot take place without water. Nutrients reach the tissues, and waste products are taken away by water. Body temperature is controlled by water through perspiration. Water is even more necessary than food.

Because excessive losses of water due to perspiration lead to fatigue and lower efficiency in shooting, the gunner should be prepared to counteract sweat losses during extended periods of competition. The pre-event meal should include enough liquid. One to three cups of water or beverage will usually be enough to ensure hydration for an athlete exercising strenuously during a hot day. Trap and skeet shooters lose water through perspiration much more gradually. Therefore, rather than consuming more water or beverage than is comfortable at meal time, the shooter should take a swallow or two whenever it is convenient.

The following are recommended beverages for the preshooting meal. Naturally, if a competitor has experienced previous discomfort from drinking a particular beverage he should avoid it.

Skim milk   Orange juice (perhaps diluted)
Apple juice   Pineapple juice (perhaps diluted)
Lemonade   Clear beef or chicken broth
Limeade   Bouillon
                            Consommé

SALT SUPPLEMENTATION

Athletes taking part in extremely vigorous activities, such as football and track in extreme hot weather, may require extra salt in the form of salt tablets. The gunner need not worry about that if food during meals is well salted.

ADJUSTMENTS FOR PROLONGED COMPETITION

In prolonged or intermittent competition, such as occurs in tournament shooting, the gunner is usually faced with problems of energy loss, dehydration, and the need for urinary and bowel elimination. These problems can be minimized by proper food and drinks selection—and by making adequate preparations ahead of time. The shooter should start by modifying his regular daily eating program forty-eight hours before shooting time.

GENERAL FATIGUE

General fatigue during a shoot may be caused simply by poor physical fitness, especially in gunners who have sit-down jobs during the week and shoot on weekends. (See section General Physical Condition.)

10 - Kinesiology in Shotgunning

WHAT IS KINESIOLOGY?

In trap and skeet shooting, the science of kinesiology—the study of body structures and their movements—involves the study of the major muscle groups and body movements utilized during the act of shooting: in particular, the muscles of the arms and shoulders, where the brunt of the shooting effort is focused, and the muscles of the legs and thighs.

The great majority of accomplished shooters employ the "high elbows" position when holding gun to shoulder. Use of this position accomplishes two important things: settling the gun butt securely into the hollow of the shoulder and allowing the gun-swinging arm to move easily, smoothly, and much further back than would be possible if a lower elbow position was used. High elbows also makes "follow through" much easier. Prove it to yourself. If you are right handed, extend your left or gun swinging arm with lowered elbow position so that your hand reaches out as far as it would if it were holding the gun forearm. Now, without changing the angulation or height of that elbow, move the upper arm at the shoulder to the left as far as it will go. Notice that your arm's backward movement quickly becomes restricted. The skeletal structure of the upper arm and shoulder has prevented a full swing. Now, return your arm to the original gun holding position, raise your elbow, and swing your arm back. You will be surprised how much further back it will go, and with what ease and smoothness. Of course, this principle applies to both arms. If the left elbow is raised in the shooting position and the right is lowered, a shooter will probably be having trouble hitting some of the targets going from left to right.

The skeletal and muscular structure of the human body also make it much more difficult to swing the gun and follow a flying target when the legs are spread too far apart. Your swing will be easier and smoother if you keep your feet closer together, that is, placed comfortably in the direction the target is expected to be broken. When your legs are spread too far apart your movements will be more restricted, due to the construction of the hip and knee joints. Again, prove it to yourself. Stand in a spread leg position and with arms up in shooting posture. Swing at an imaginary target. Note that the muscles and joints not only prevent an easy and complete swing, but appear to be fighting each other. Change your posture. Bring your knees closer together. Lean forward a bit with left leg slightly bent at the knee and the right leg straight. Most of the body weight is taken by the left leg. Swing your body and arms at an imaginary flying target. Your swing will be much easier in this position.

Little idiosyncrasies of form and movement are indulged in by all gunners. But it is an unwise or uninformed trap or skeet shooter who tries to fight against the natural restrictions of movement controlled by the bones and muscles of his body.

A WORD ABOUT EXERCISE

In addition to properly positioning the bones and muscles for maximum freedom of movement, the shooter should also be concerned with developing his muscles for endurance, so that several rounds of shooting will not bring on undue fatigue. The following exercises are designed to provide a simple yet effective regimen for improving a shooter's strength and endurance.

In a number of the exercises the use of weights is recommended. How much weight to use will depend on the size and strength of the individual. Weights should be heavy enough so that a certain amount of effort is required to complete the exercise; if completed too easily, little benefit will be gained. After several weeks of exercising, the amount of weight should be slightly increased, so that it continues to be a burden to move or lift. As modern day weight lifters put it "no pain—no gain." However, since the shooter is primarily seeking to develop endurance and not great strength, I recommend that the exercise not be pushed to a point of maximum discomfort. Work out the system that is best for you.

The weight may be a "store-bought" cast iron dumbbell, or something as common as a brick or even a box of shells. For small-structured persons a weight of three to five pounds is adequate for a start. A box of 12-gauge shells (2.8 pounds) will do. For the bigger persons or athletes, ten pounds would be good for a starter. The weight should be easy to hold and balance in one hand. A lighter weight may be used for particularly difficult exercises. For example, a box of shells might be an appropriate weight for the wrist curl (Exercise 7) whereas a brick or a ten-pound weight might work better for the overhead press (Exercise 3).

Each exercise should be exerted deliberately and fully. Training should start slowly and particular exercises should be separated by muscle groups. For example, all of the shoulder exercises should not follow one another; otherwise the shoulder may become sore, preventing the exercises from

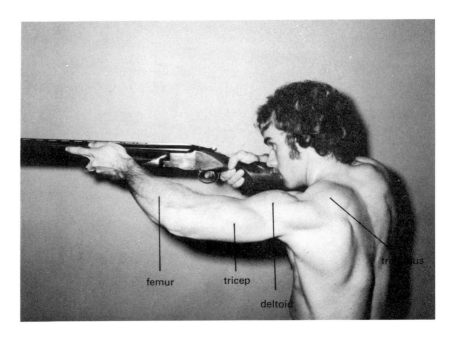

femur   tricep   deltoid   tr...us

The muscles used in shotgunning and a simple exercise (below, right) to develop them, as described in the text.

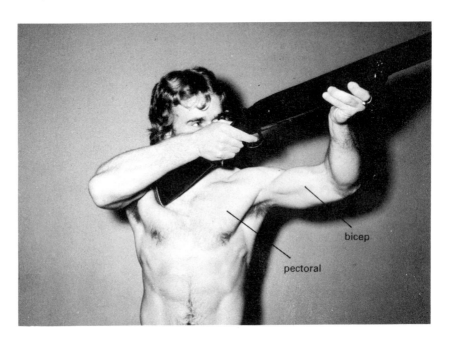

bicep

pectoral

being done correctly. Do a shoulder exercise, then one for the other parts of the body before returning to do another for the shoulders. If one set of ten repetitions is insufficient, do up to three sets of ten repetitions. Again, start moderately and always alternate exercises.

The exercises should be disciplined. Get accustomed to performing them at the same time each day—before breakfast, for example. They need not be done *every* day, however; every other day will suffice. If you feel that the effort of planned exercising is too much of a bother, then at least do as many push-ups as possible every morning. It is also important to note that just as "running is the best exercise for running," so is shouldering and swinging an empty gun twenty-five times every day an excellent exercise for developing endurance; if performed in front of a mirror, it will help your form.

Finally, a word of caution: muscular endurance cannot be achieved in one day. Exercise should continue at least every second day during the shooting season. If you exercise daily, give your body a rest the day before a shoot.

TEN EASY AT-HOME EXERCISES TO IMPROVE YOUR SHOOTING ENDURANCE

HEAD AND NECK

When standing in proper shooting position on the field, the head should be held as upright as is comfortably possible, with the gunstock being raised to the face, instead of the head being lowered to the stock. Thus, since the head and neck should do no more than flow with the rest of the body movements, no major muscle-building exercises are recommended. Many shooters, however, suffer from fatigue in these areas because of tension. Relaxation is the key. Facial muscles should be loose, eyes comfortably open, not squinted. The jaw should be relaxed, without the teeth being clenched.

For the neck, stretching exercises are useful. Keeping the shoulders square, rotate the head, tipping as far forward, sideways, and backwards as possible. Complete five rotations in each direction, clockwise and counterclockwise.

SHOULDERS

The shoulders, a major area of fatigue, support much of the weight of the gun and contribute greatly to the swing and follow through. When the arms are extended and raised the deltoids (shoulder muscles) and trapezius (the muscles between the deltoids, across the lower back of the neck) raise the arms and lift the shoulders. The following exercises will help develop those muscles.

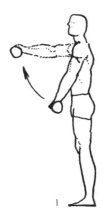

Exercise 1

Stand erect with the weight held in one hand (knuckles upward) at your side. Keeping your arm straight, slowly lift the weight, out in front of your body, up to eye level. Then, slowly lower it to the original position. Follow the same procedure ten times with each arm.

Exercise 2

Stand erect. Hold the weight in front of your belt buckle and then raise it slowly and vertically until the top of your hand reaches your chin; keep the elbow higher than the hand at all times. Return the weight slowly to original position. Repeat ten times for each arm.

Exercise 3

Hold the weight close to shoulder. Slowly press it straight overhead to full arm extension, then lower it to the starting position. Repeat ten times for each arm.

The chest muscles, called pectorals, do not come into play very much during shooting, but they do draw the arms together at the gun.

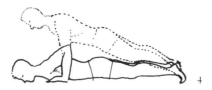

Exercise 4

The best exercise for the chest is a "push-up." This drill is also beneficial in developing the upper arm and shoulder muscles, which are so important in reducing gun-handling fatigue. Twenty repetitions should suffice.

UPPER ARM

The function of the muscle group called triceps, located along the back side of the upper arm between shoulder and elbow, is to extend the arm at the elbow. This action allows the arms to be outstretched to the gun. The triceps may seem to play an insignificant role in gun handling, but they are one of the first muscles to feel fatigue when the gun is being mounted. The development of the triceps is especially important to gunners who have a tendency to hold the gun in position for a longer period of time than necessary before calling for the target.

Exercise 5

Hold the weight straight above your head; grasp extended elbow with free hand and hold firmly, thereby preventing movement between elbow and shoulder. Flexing only at the elbow, bring the weight down to the back of the shoulder; then, still holding the elbow with the free hand, extend the lower arm to the upright position, by this means bringing the weight above your head. Repeat ten times for each arm.

The biceps, the muscles opposing the triceps, are located on the inside of the upper arm. They flex the arm at the elbow, consequently drawing the arm inward. Biceps should be in good condition to hold the gun firmly against shoulder.

Exercise 6

Stand erect with elbow pinned to hip bone. Bend your arm at the elbow and bring weight up to shoulder. Then slowly lower weight to original position. Repeat ten times with each arm.

FOREARM

The forearm muscles, located on the topside of the lower arm, between elbow and hand, are the extensors. They support and extend the wrist and hand. These muscles bend the wrist backwards, thereby allowing your left hand (if you are right handed) to remain flush against the gun at about a 135° angle with your forearm. The same applies to your trigger hand. Some of the gun's weight is also supported by the forearm muscles.

Exercise 7

While sitting in an arm chair, place forearm (holding the weight) on the arm rest, palm down. Curl the weight upward and backward. Move only the hand and wrist and keep the forearm in place. Repeat ten times for each hand.

In the clay target games the waist is involved in much of the swing and follow-through movements. The muscles of the lower back and abdomen should be relaxed and capable of smooth, maximum movement from side to side. The following exercises are also recommended for loosening up before shooting time, especially on a cold day. Do not work on Exercise 8 immediately before shooting; allow about a half hour before you are scheduled to be on station.

Exercise 8

Stand with arms fully extended and legs spread to the sides. Keep your knees straight. Touch the left hand to the right foot, keeping the right arm extended up and backward. Straighten up and then touch the right hand to the left foot, while keeping the left arm extended up and backward. Repeat ten times to each side.

Exercise 9

Stand with your feet spread apart at the same distance they would be if you are on station in shooting position. With arms fully extended out to the sides at shoulder height, swing them 180° from side to side. Note that as you complete a swing to one side, your knee will be bent slightly as it is in shooting position.

LEGS

Straining thighs that are not in condition can be a source of general fatigue in shooting. People who indulge in squatting, leg spreading, or excessive leaning on the trap or skeet field are especially prone to fatigue, though they may not realize it. Any bending of the legs puts tension on the muscles of the front of the upper leg called the quadriceps.

The shooter's classical stance in clay target shooting is basically an upright position. Many gunners, however, bend their forward knee in various degrees, causing energy-consuming strain. The next exercise will benefit any shooter, but it is a must with squatters, leaners and leg spreaders.

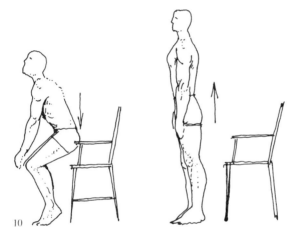

Exercise 10

Stand erect in front of a chair as if you are about to sit in it. With a weight in each hand to keep balance, and your back held as upright as possible, bend at the knees until your buttocks just touch the seat of the chair, then straighten up. Do not take tension off the thighs by sitting down between flexions. Repeat twenty times.

11 - Eyes and Sighting

The advice given to new shooters by knowledgeable instructors is to shoot with both eyes open, if possible. Using both eyes gives the gunner greater peripheral vision, making him better equipped to pick up the target sooner and to judge its apparent direction and speed. Using two eyes will also prevent excessive strain on the sighting eye. Moreover, the gunner who uses only one eye will be inclined to aim at the clay bird rather than pointing at it. The shotgun is not meant to be aimed at the target; it should be pointed.

Some instructors maintain that it is possible to become an expert shotgunner by sighting with one eye, pointing out that some of the great tournament champions employ the one-eye method. It is true that a few of the really outstanding shotgun shooters close one eye voluntarily. However, many of them do so because of permanent eye injuries or because the master or dominant eye is not the one they use to sight along the gun barrel. For example, if a right handed shooter's left eye is the master eye it must be closed so that the gunner will not be inadvertently sighting with the master eye instead of the one that is actually looking down the barrel. If you have no eye problems, by all means try to get accustomed to shooting with two eyes open. If your master eye is not the one nearest to the sighting plane of your gun you can still become a good shooter by closing it while on station. Gunners in such a situation find it easier to block off that eye from working by covering the eye glass lens with tape. However, this practice invites fatigue in the eye that is doing all the looking. The covered eye should therefore have a "flip-up" covering, so that both eyes can be used for general viewing when the gunner is not actually on station.

If you are a right-handed shooter and your left eye is the master, you might want to switch to left-handed shooting in order to shoot with both eyes open. But such a switch is simply too awkward for most people.

MASTER EYE

As stated previously, when shooting with both eyes open, one eye usually dominates the actual alignment and coordination of aiming the shotgun. That eye is the "master eye," sometimes referred to as the "dominant eye."

All shotgunners should know which is their master eye. If you are a beginner and you have not been instructed on how to check for your master eye, you can do it yourself. The procedure is simple. With both eyes open point your right hand finger at some object and keep it there. Close your left eye. If the finger remains on that target, it means that your right eye is master. If your finger moves out of alignment with the object, the left eye is master. If your left eye seems to be the dominant eye, you can check the drill by looking at the same object, only this time close the right eye. If your left eye is really your master eye it will remain accurately pointed to the object.

SIGHTING AT A TARGET

Your eyes cannot focus up close and at a distance at the same time. Next time you pick up your gun, point it at a stationary object. You will note that if your eyes are concentrated on the target, only about the front one-third of your gun barrel is in focus. In other words the portion closest to your eyes is blurred or out of focus, but the tip of the forward sight is clearly seen.

Now, to get to the real nub of "pointing" a shotgun. Use all of the sighting plane of your gun that is clearly defined and ignore everything else that is out of focus or blurry. This is the reason why the expert trap and skeet shooters do not use the center bead of the shotgun for sighting at the target. The trick is to ignore the middle bead, and sight off the tip of the gun, that is, the forward bead. Actually, the shooter's eyes serve as the near sight. This method of sighting brings your natural binocular vision more easily into use. By ignoring the center bead the left eye is put into action (even though your right eye is the master); it sees under the barrel, even though both eyes are viewing over the barrel. And because the vision of the left eye is not blocked by the gun barrel hoisted to your right shoulder, it has an unobstructed initial viewing of the target; it therefore assists greatly in estimating the speed and angle of its flight.

The middle bead of a shotgun should never be used for pointing the gun at target. If the beginner uses the middle bead for anything besides checking the *initial alignment* for gun canting and proper shouldering, he is ruining his chances of learning the easy method of "pointing" a shotgun.

SHOOTING GLASSES AND SUNGLASSES

There are three highly important reasons why shooting glasses must be worn:

1. To protect the eyes from broken target chips;

2. As an aid in sighting the target;

3. To prevent exposure to glare that accelerates body fatigue and contributes to headache.

Any eyeglasses are better than none as a protection against bits of broken clay targets. However, shooting glasses are recommended. They are heat treated to resist impact, they ride high on the nose, and they protect a wide area around the eye.

Sunglasses can be purchased in an exhausting array of prices, sizes, styles, and colors—all the way from the drugstore-counter variety at a couple dollars a pair, to the really fine impact resistant, shooting glasses (produced by Bausch and Lomb), which have photochromic lenses that get darker as the sun gets brighter. The drugstore type of glasses are useless; all they do is block out a very small percentage of the total light. The shooter should buy the best shooting glasses he can afford, because long exposure to shooting under bright skies may cause not only eye strain and fatigue, but retinal damage as well.

The most practical color is natural gray, because it creates little or no color distortion. Another good color is sage green, which permits the passage of those colors that the eye best perceives while restricting or reducing the passage of other colors in the visual spectrum. Yellow lenses aid in improving contrast on gray, cloudy or rainy days.

Plastic lenses, which have come into general popular use in recent years, will filter out ultraviolet rays but do not protect against infrared, the heat ray. Only lenses made of glass are used in good sunglasses. For shooting, sunglasses should have strong, comfortable frames; plastic types generally do not. If you wear prescription eyeglasses for shooting, the lenses should have enough surface area to be placed in the regular, shooting-type sunglass frames to give good glare protection.

Clip-on sunglasses can cause problems. Because of the added weight they tend to keep sliding down the nose, and the extra pair of lens surfaces create confusing reflections.

When you are purchasing a good pair of sunglasses, hold them under an overhead fluorescent light and catch the reflection on the inside of each lens, one at a time. Move the glasses a bit so that the reflection travels across the lens. If wiggling or waves show on the image, the lenses are faulty and will create eye strain. Don't buy them.

Trap and skeet matches and tournaments are usually not cancelled on rainy days. Water spotting the eyeglass lenses may be a problem. Glass sprays are available which are designed to repel water by forming a tough film over the lenses, keeping them reasonably clear. The film also prevents fogging from body heat. Spray the lenses both inside and out.

EYES AND SMOKE

Eyes not only work best when they have had adequate rest through sleep, but they also require clean air. Late-night card games, where people are smoking, will add greatly to eye strain in the next day's shooting. Similarly, shooters who go from a smoky club house directly to the shooting fields are expecting too much from their eyes. Under such conditions the eyes will not perform at their best and the shooter's scores will drop.

12 - Flinching

According to Webster's dictionary, the word flinch means "to shrink from or as if from physical pain: wince: to tense the muscles involuntarily in fear." Flinching is an affliction that suddenly develops, adversely affecting the capabilities of skeet and trap veterans as well as neophytes. Flinching prevents a smooth or continuous swing. It may cause slight hesitancy in older shooters, and with young or new shooters it is often responsible for stopping gun swing completely at the moment the trigger is pulled. Obviously, flinching is highly detrimental to the attainment of high trap and skeet scores.

It is an important discovery when a shooter finds that flinching has begun to be a problem. But what causes the problem? Perhaps my definition of flinching, as applied to shooting, may lead to an answer: "flinching is an involuntary physical or mental reaction brought about by the anticipation of pain or discomfort." If the shooter consciously or unconsciously expects bodily inconvenience it is impossible for him to concentrate totally on shooting the target. In order to put the mind at ease it is necessary to discover the cause of the flinching.

When a beginner flinches upon pulling the trigger, squinting or totally closing the eyes, it is usually in anticipation of a bruised shoulder. The instructor should check for proper gun butt placement in the shoulder pocket. Raising the elbows will usually rectify the problem. Also, the gun butt should be equipped with a recoil pad. Another problem that may cause flinching with the new shooter is ill-fitting ear protectors that do not shield the inner ear from the gun blast. In some cases, flinching will be caused by the gun stock hitting the bottom of the ear muffs.

When flinching suddenly becomes a problem with experienced shooters, diagnosis is not so simple. Most professional gun writers suggest that the shooter examine his equipment thoroughly. Is the gun stock too high? Does the gun fit properly? Is the recoil pad right for the gun? Have you changed from light to heavy clothes, or the other way around? Did you change guns? If so, is the trigger pull heavier than on your other gun? Any one of these factors could be the reason for the veteran shooter to suddenly start flinching.

But there is another possibility—one that I have never seen discussed in any periodical: that flinching can be the result of fatigue. I strongly believe that fatigue can have a significant affect on the normal capabilities of an experienced shooter. Therefore, when trying to help a shooter affected by flinching, the first thing I do is check for symptoms of fatigue. First I look for arm fatigue, which, in my estimation, is the prime cause of flinching. If the arms have had no meaningful exercise in the couple of weeks before shooting, then suddenly are put to work holding the gun and swinging it during a couple of rounds of trap or skeet, they will rebel and actually tremble slightly, without it being noticed by the gunner. Tired muscles, which also cause flinching, commonly occur among people over thirty years of age, but arm fatigue may cause flinching in anyone, regardless of age. Eyestrain, defective sunglasses, or too much coffee drinking before a shoot, are but a few more of the likely causes of flinching. The chapters concerned with Kinesiology, Physiology, Psychology, and Nutrition will suggest other possible causes of flinching.

13 - Shooter's Conduct

Because potentially lethal firearms are involved in recreational shooting, the conduct of those participating is a matter of concern to all those present. Safety rules must be rigidly obeyed and enforced. Some behavior patterns are set by the rules of trap and skeet, while others are governed by nothing more than common sense, courtesy, and good manners. Basically, the rules of conduct fall into three categories: safety, courtesy, and sportsmanship.

SAFETY

There can be no compromise where safety is concerned. New trap or skeet shooters should be thoroughly familiar with the ATA or NSSA rule book and should pay special attention to those sections dealing with safety, before attempting the first round of shooting. Also, a newcomer should not be permitted to join a squad unless an arrangement has been made with a veteran shooter or instructor to be at his side at each station, to coach him on matters of safety.

Gun safety begins before you reach the trap or skeet field. As soon as you remove your gun from its guncase, whether at your car or at the clubhouse, the action should be opened immediately. The gun should be carried with its breech open until you are actually on station and ready to shoot. Never place a shell in the gun until you are on the shooting post. The loaded gun must be kept pointed in a direction that will not threaten injury or death to shooters, field personnel, or spectators. An important safety rule concerns both the shooter whose gun is loaded and ready to shoot but who then faces a delay, such as equipment breakdown, and the shooter who arrives at station out of turn. The gun must be pointed outward and the shells must be extracted *before* the gunner turns to walk off station.

Every gun club should have the following rules posted, in easily readable letters and in a conspicuous spot:

1. TREAT EVERY GUN AS IF LOADED
2. KEEP MUZZLE POINTING SAFELY AT ALL TIMES
3. DO NOT LOAD GUN UNTIL READY TO SHOOT
4. MAKE SURE AMMO GAUGE IS SAME AS GUN
5. KEEP ACTION OPEN WHEN NOT SHOOTING

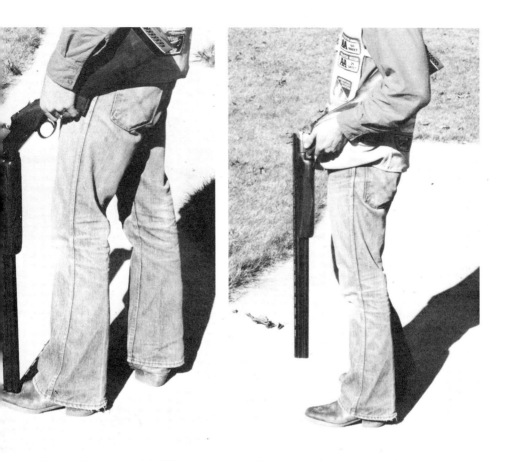

Acceptable ways of holding and of carrying guns when not actually shooting.

Again, I warn the newcomer. Your mistakes or omissions in the shooting program will be expected. But ignorance or casual disregard of safety rules will not be tolerated by fellow gunners. Read the book of rules concerning gun safety and shooting procedures before going out on the field for the first time. *Better to be safe than sorry.*

COURTESY

Courtesy in trap and skeet shooting involves nothing more than good manners and concern for your fellow gunners. Starting at the club house, don't touch another person's gun without the owner's permission. Don't place your gun on a table; racks are always provided. Don't dry fire or follow

107

Acceptable ways of holding and of carrying guns when not actually shooting.

targets with your gun at any time on the field or on the walks outside the immediate shooting field. Don't talk in a loud voice; better yet, don't talk at all when a member of your squad is on station ready to shoot. Some shooters are extremely sensitive to distractions while they are trying to concentrate on the forthcoming target. Do not offer advice. Comments like "You were behind the target," or "above the target," do more harm than good. Only experienced coaches should give instructions, and only when asked to do so. Because you are a new shooter does not mean that you have the right to take more time than is required at the shooting station. Don't hold your gun to shoulder position for more time than is necessary. It wastes time and contributes to fatigue. Also, don't swing your gun back and forth several times before calling for the target. This sort of action makes you look ridiculous, and the other shooters in the squad are certain to be annoyed at you for

taking too much time. Above all, if you miss the clay bird, don't stand on station groaning or leave the station muttering, swearing, or shaking your head. And certainly don't tell the next man coming up on station why you missed. Not only is such conduct objectionable to your fellow shooters, but it makes you appear immature. If you miss, be a gentleman. Step out of the station smartly, keep your mouth shut and your thoughts to yourself. To me, the most obnoxious of all prima donnas is the shooter who smokes while waiting his turn to shoot, and then casually flips his live butt onto the field or grinds it under his shoe before mounting his gun to his shoulder.

SPORTSMANSHIP

Sportsmanship in gunning is no different than it is in any other sport. The chief example of poor behavior in this respect is the shooter who disputes

Acceptable ways of holding and of carrying guns when not actually shooting.

the referee's call, either on his own shots or those of another squad member. Even worse is the shooter who tries to browbeat the puller into changing his decision from a "miss" to a "hit." Another type of poor sportsmanship is the shooter who hotly demands that the machines and the target flight be

110

A most tactless and disconcerting disregard for safety rules is swinging a gun within a group of people. This candid photo illustrates a fault that is a common sight at gun facilities.

One of the worst breeches of etiquette and disregard for safety rules is to dry fire at targets while a squad is shooting. This candid photo shows a person by the gun rack following targets while the squad is shooting at Station 7.

111

checked in the middle of a shoot. Target flight is checked before the shoot, usually early in the day when wind influence is at a minimum. A sudden gust of wind may or may not be the reason for a miss, but it is no reason to call for a target check, thereby disrupting the rest of the squad's shooting. If the target throwing machine is malfunctioning it will be obvious to everyone, including the referee.

RULES AND REGULATIONS

All official clay target games held nationally or internationally follow specific rules and regulations designed by organizations and associations. American trap is guided by the Amateur Trap Association (ATA). American skeet is directed by the National Skeet Shooting Association (NSSA). International Trap and International Skeet are governed by the International Shooting Union (ISU) with the U.S. representative being the National Rifle Association (NRA). The addresses of these organizations can be found in the Appendix.

14 - Learning to Shoot

FINDING AN INSTRUCTOR

Most newcomers to clay target shooting usually become interested in the sport through friends who are gunning enthusiasts. Many have also been drawn to it when presented with the opportunity in school or college, either through courses or through recreation and club sport programs. Rod and gun clubs that support gunnery programs naturally draw portions of their memberships into skeet and trap shooting.

If you are interested in becoming a trap or skeet shooter but haven't had the benefit of any of the above situations, you have three avenues open to you. You can join a club that offers trap or skeet as a regular activity; pay a professional instructor, or do it yourself. If you join a club, you will soon discover that many shooters welcome the chance to instruct or coach you. Beware! Every shooter, even the one with only a few weeks experience, has a craving to teach a new shooter. Whether the club has certain regulars who do the instructing, or the opportunities for learning are informal, I suggest you do the following. If there is an instructors' program, observe the instructors in action. If not, watch the veteran club members who have reputations for being good shooters. Take note of those who shoot with an easy, relaxed form, who do not squat, lean forward in a strained manner, or spread their feet wide apart. The shooter who uses an exaggerated stance is also likely to call for a target by shouting "Yaaa!" or "Hupp!" or some other noise resembling a bear's growl or a pig's grunt. A few such exhibitionists may shoot good scores, but only because they have been participating in trap and skeet for years, with the result that they find it practically impossible to change their idiosyncratic styles. These shooters will have good intentions, but they will teach you their way of shooting—a style that has been developed for the benefit of the audience rather than for purposes of good form. When you have located an experienced shooter with good form and a calm style, approach him after he has finished shooting, and ask him if he could spare the time to instruct you in a round of skeet. The best way to learn is to start at the easier stations, but this may not be practical since the club may have imposed time restrictions on regularly scheduled squad shooting.

Unquestionably, the most productive way of learning trap and skeet, if you can afford it, is to hire a "pro." Pros are usually available at large gun clubs. The pro approach has many advantages, including access to a field where no one else is shooting. Here again, if more than one instructor is available choose the one who is relaxed and calm; he will have more patience with you.

DO IT YOURSELF

In the "do it yourself" approach, the learner can go a long way towards becoming a trap and skeet shooter, although eventually the help of an experienced shooter will be necessary. These are the facts and procedures to take into consideration:

1. Read this book from cover to cover.

2. Send letters to the Shooting Promotions Managers at Winchester-Western (New Haven, Conn.), Remington Arms (Stratford, Conn.), and the National Shooting Sports Foundation (Riverside, Conn.). Ask the respective managers to send you their brochures describing methods of shooting trap and skeet. Included in these publications will be descriptions of trap and skeet fields and the procedures for shooting the clay target games.

3. Visit the trap and skeet fields. Observe the shooting procedures and watch how the gunners position themselves in shooting order. Note how they hold their guns open when not shooting and how no gun is loaded until the shooter steps on station, ready to shoot. Be aware that the loaded gun is *always* pointed to the open field. Also, notice that no talking takes place when a person is on station ready to call for a target.

4. Study the stances the shooters assume when at station. Disregard the squatters, leaners, and leg spreaders. Be sure to observe foot position. The principal point here is that although the gun is pointed towards the trap house the feet are comfortably aligned in the direction toward which the target is expected to break. Note that the good shooters will invariably hold their elbows high when the gun is shouldered. (This helps to pocket the gun butt in the hollow of the shoulder and facilitates easier gun swing and follow-through.)

5. When the squad is through with a round of shooting, ask the person reloading the target machines to show you the machines and how they work.

6. Now to the gun and ammunition. The ammunition is no problem. Trap or skeet shells—or "ammo"—can be bought at all gun clubs and sport shops. Later, when you become experienced, you can learn to load your own shells and save money. But don't buy a gun until you learn to shoot and become familiar with guns. Trap and skeet require special types of guns. They can be rented for a nominal fee at gun clubs, or your instructor will loan you his. When you become proficient, you will want to buy your own.

Aside from the satisfaction of owning your own shotgun, your scores will be better if you always shoot with the same gun. The most popular clay target model—and the one recommended—is the auto-loader (also called semi-automatic). Beginners should stay away from the slide action or pump guns. Refer to the section of this book that describes the four types of shotguns. Also review the portions that deal with gun fit.

If you are a hunter, you have obviously passed the gun safety test before you obtained a license. Therefore, it is possible that by following the above directions you can actually "do it yourself." But I strongly suggest that you make every effort to have an experienced shooter next to you on the field for the first couple or three times you shoot.

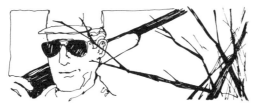

Smart gunners know that good, impact-resistant shooting glasses are an absolute safety requirement whether on the range or in the field. They also know that on sunny days green or gray lenses will keep their eyes fresh and untired by glare, helping them get on target faster, while yellow glasses which brighten up the landscape will sharpen their shooting in dim or fading light. They know too that by wearing shooting glasses they avoid the risk of being painfully "twigged" in the eye while hunting in brushy cover so they never go afield without them.

EYE PROTECTION

It is absolutely imperative that eyeglasses be worn during shooting, first as a safety precaution and second as an aid to shooting during bright or sunny days. At times, the sharp chips from the broken clay travel from the path of the flying target and pose a danger to the unprotected eye. Also, it takes only one pellet, ricocheted from the hard clay surface of the target, to cause serious injury to the eye. The incoming targets at Stations 1, 7, and 8 are the ones that present the greatest chance of a piece of the target hitting the eye or face either of the shooter or of another member of the squad. Regular prescription glasses and ordinary sunglasses may serve the purpose, although specially designed shooting glasses are recommended (see Chapters 9 and 11). No shooter, whether learner or expert, should ever venture onto the field shooting without adequate eye protection.

Heavy, repeated exposure to the sound of shot-guns, center fire rifles or handguns causes permanent hearing damage which may not be discovered until it's too late. Whether muff type, plug, valve or custom molded insert, every target shooter can find a kind of hearing guard he'll find comfortable and easy to wear.

EAR PROTECTION

Ear protection is just as necessary as eye protection, even though the injury is cumulative and not as sudden and dramatic as having a piece of the clay target hit the eye. Noise pollution may affect the hearing so gradually that a shooter may not realize that permanent impairment of his hearing is taking place. Young shooters, the teenagers especially, may believe that they are tough enough to discard protective ear devices while shooting, but they are mistaken. Many shooters have suffered some degree of hearing loss because they failed to wear ear protectors; some actually brag about it. But once the thin membrane of the ear drum is damaged by repetitive gun blasts, it will never return to normal.

It is also important to wear ear protectors when you are a spectator standing close enough to shotgun firing to feel blast discomfort.

In a pinch, if you lose your ear protectors, a piece of rolled cotton will help; it is better than nothing. An inexpensive commercial ear plug, used in some factories to cut down noise, is simply constructed of a plastic sponge-like substance. When squeezed it fits into the ear, and moments later expands to fill the ear canal. These are not easy to find, however.

Ear protectors are advertised in all the trap and skeet periodicals. The gun department of your sporting goods store certainly carries them.

The three standard types of ear protectors are:

a. The so-called earmuffs, cup-like devices that cover the entire ear. They are held in place by a metal or plastic band that reaches over the head from ear to ear. They are available in various designs. Some shooters object to this type of ear covering, finding that because of the way they position their head on the gun, the upper edge of the stock hits the lower part of the muff when the gun is shouldered. This is particularly a problem with shooters who use a gun with a Monte Carlo stock.

b. Another type, known as "Sonic Ear Valves" are widely used by shotgunners. They are of a flexible, rubber-like composition and are designed to fit anyone's ears. Inside they contain a mechanical diaphragm, which is activated by the noise level.

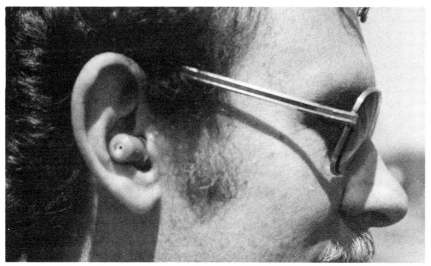

The "Sonic Ear Valves" are widely used by shotgunners for ear protection.

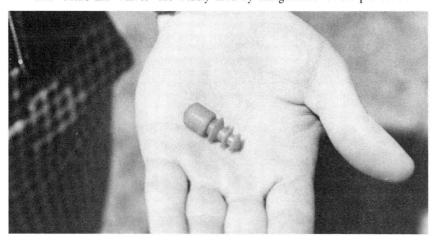

c. Special, individually molded ear plugs, usually obtainable from hearing-aid specialists, are preferred by some shooters. These plugs are formed when a dough-like substance placed in the ear, solidifies into a flexible, rubbery agent that retains its shape. It adopts the exact form of the ear canal.

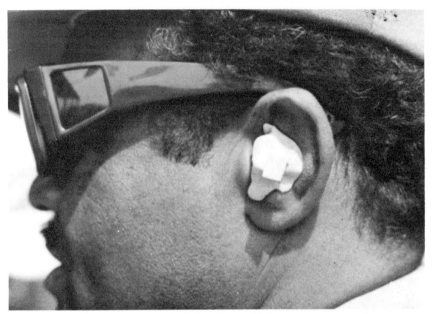

Some shooters claim that the individually molded ear plugs give the best ear protection.

HEADWEAR

Young gunners, when shooting, usually shun headwear. They disregard, or do not recognize, the fact that a wide-brim hat or a peaked cap can be a benefit in several ways, helping to shield the eyes from sun glare, protect the face from pieces of chipped targets, and reduce chances of heat fatigue in the summer. In winter, a hat or cap helps retain body heat.

SHOOTING VEST

All trap and skeet shooters should wear a shooting vest or a loosely belted shell pouch. The vest has a leather shoulder pad that prevents gun butt slippage, and also helps to cushion the effects of gun recoil. The shell pouch,

The "International vest" is specifically designed for those events where the gun butt is brought down to hip level before calling for a target. Here Brad Simmons relaxes while waiting his turn to shoot.

on the other hand, is lighter in weight, and does not drag on the shoulders, as do the shell-stuffed pockets of the shooting vest. The pouch is held in place over the hip by a separate belt (not the same one used to hold up the trousers). If you cannot immediately afford a vest, buy a shell pouch; any old belt will do to hold it in place. There is nothing more distracting and frustrating to a shooter than having to wait while a fellow shooter goes searching for a shell in the tight pockets of a pair of body-form bluejeans.

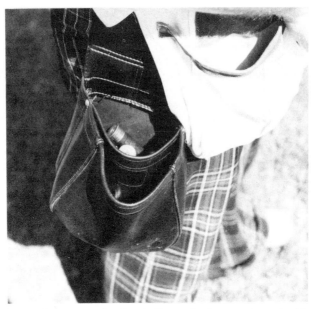

Some shooters prefer the shell pouch that rests on the hip because the weight of the shells does not drag on the shooting shoulder. One pocket in the double compartment pouch serves as a container for empty hulls intended for reloading.

HAIR CONTROL

Equally exasperating, to the shooter as well as to the other members of the squad, is the frequent need of both male and female longhairs to brush the hair out of their eyes before shooting. If you have long hair and absolutely cannot wear a hat, use a bandana, or a sweat band, or a rope, or anything else that will keep your hair under control.

FOOTWEAR

Beginners, but also many experienced shooters, especially teenagers, often give little thought to the type of shoes they wear on the shooting field. Use common sense. In excessive heat, wear shoes that have some substance to the soles. Do not wear basketball or tennis shoes. Sun heat, absorbed by concrete or asphalt walks, will penetrate thin soles and may contribute to your general heat fatigue. In winter, wear substantial heavy boot-like shoes, insulated if possible. The discomfort of cold feet will not help your score.

Warmth and comfortable clothes that allow free movement, especially of the arms, are the basic requirements for enjoyable winter shooting. A gunner whose mind is on his cold feet or freezing hands will not shoot well. Light weight insulated underwear like that worn by skiers is a necessity. A turtleneck sweater is a blessing when the wind breezes over the snow. A down or woolen hat should be used. And a pair of heavy boots that are either insulated, felt-lined, or rubber bottom leather top must be worn. In very cold weather the jacket should be one of the many styles of nylon-insulated types. Stay clear of the bulky, slippery surface kind unless a non-slip shoulder pad has been sewn on. Some shooters wear a regular shooting vest over the jacket, but obviously a larger size is required than the regular summer one. A pair of leather insulated gloves complete the outfit. Some shooters take off the trigger hand glove when ready to shoot. Needless to say dark glasses are imperative against the glaring light of sun on snow.

121

HOW MUCH DOES IT COST?

The general opinion among non-shooters is that clay target shooting is a rich man's sport. That may have been the case years ago, but not today. The options available, in terms of financial outlay, run from inexpensive hand-trap shooting, to the moderate cost of a couple of rounds of trap or skeet per week, to the fairly large amounts of money that highly competitive gunners spend on guns, shells, registration fees, and travel.

Buying a gun.

The least expensive, and in many cases the most enjoyable, type of clay bird shooting, involves father-and-son, father-and-daughter, or the entire family, on a day's outing, for which they may be equipped with a 20-gauge gun, ammunition that has been loaded at home, a case of clay targets, and either a hand trap or a portable target-throwing mechanism.

A case of 135 targets and a couple boxes of hand-loaded shells cost far less than the food in a picnic outing for a family of four. A hand trap that will serve for years costs about the same as a half-pound of freeze-dried coffee. The financial output for a portable, target-throwing machine is less than that for a pair of shoes. The shoes will be long gone before the machine becomes inoperative. Ear muffs cost less than a tank of gas for a car. And shell pouches can be home made from discarded women's pocketbooks, appropriately modified and equipped with an old belt. A second-hand 20-gauge shotgun can be an inexpensive Christmas gift for someone in the family, and everyone can use it!

If the newcomer to the clay target games wants to shoot recreationally and to enter into low-key competition on week-ends, the original financial requirement for gun, glasses, ear muffs and vest or belt-pouch are insignificant in proportion to the many years of service they will give. The gun is an investment that can be recouped. At today's (1977) prices, a good trap or skeet gun is obtainable for about $300. Second-hand guns can be purchased for much less. The great majority of week-end trap and skeet shooters load their own shells for about one-half the cost of a "store-bought" box. Also, most regular gunners join a club, thereby becoming eligible for reduced rates in target fees. Some clubs also buy the shell components in huge lots and sell them to members at discount prices. Using these methods, a round of skeet (shells and targets) costs less than the price of a movie. From then on, the cost depends on how intensely the shooter pursues competitive shooting, how much time he can give to travelling, and how much he can spend.

PART III
KNOWING YOUR EQUIPMENT

15 - Gunology

There is a tremendous amount of literature—books, pamphlets, brochures and magazine articles—specifically concerned with guns, their history, development, use, performance, and selection. This material is readily available to any shooter. The following review of basic gunology (the study of guns) is geared to serve as a guide for beginners as well as for instructors and coaches. Because this volume is primarily concerned with the clay target games, the information mostly encompasses trap and skeet guns and associated items.

NOT A WEAPON

One of my particular peeves is to hear a person, especially an instructor or coach, refer to a trap or skeet gun as "the weapon." Such terminology is a holdover from military rifle instruction, where such a reference was perfectly appropriate. Trap and skeet guns are *not* weapons, but *recreational* or *sporting firearms*, and they should be referred to as such.

A BIT OF HISTORY

Today's shotguns are breech-loaders. But it was only a little more than a hundred years ago that all firearms were muzzle loaders. Various inventors tried to develop a breech-loading gun but all attempts were unsuccessful because such arms leaked powder at the breech, weakening the charge and, more often than not, burning the hand or face of the shooter. Breech-loading first became practical about 1860 with the advent of fixed ammunition having metallic cartridge cases to act as gas seals.

In early firearms—arquebuses and blunderbusses, and later muskets and fowling pieces—the inside of the barrel was smooth. These "smooth bores" used round lead balls, lead shot, or fragmented lead scraps, and were loaded through the muzzle.

The earliest muzzle-loaders were fired by a slow match put to a touchhole at the breech. The next development was the use of steel and flint to produce the sparks that set off the charge. One of the models that employed the steel

127

and flint arrangement was a "wheel-lock," which was wound with a key. Another, a more practical design, was called the "flint-lock." It was from these early guns that the term "lock, stock, and barrel" originated as an expression of completeness. Flintlocks were "primed" by fine powder held in a "pan," into which were struck the sparks caused by the contact of flint and steel. When, at times, the priming powder jolted away from the "touchhole" and fired off with a flash that failed to set off the powder charge in the barrel, the result was called a "flash in the pan."

THE DIFFERENCE BETWEEN A RIFLE AND A SHOTGUN

Gun historians believe that some gunsmith in Germany discovered that grooves in a barrel afforded tighter fitting bullets to be rammed down easily. And if the grooves were spiraled, causing the bullet to spin in flight, shooting accuracy was greatly improved. This process of grooving the barrels was called rifling—hence the name "rifle."

All rifles have spiraled grooves in the lining of the barrels and shoot bullets. Shotguns, on the other hand, are smooth bores and fire shotshells. The bullet is a single piece of lead that requires precision aiming at the target. The shotshell contains a number of small, perfectly round pellets, or shot, which spread over a certain area so that flying targets can be hit. And the gun is pointed, not aimed, at the moving target. Just as bullets come in a variety of types, so do shotshells vary in strength of powder and size of shot. The width of the shot pattern at an effective distance also varies. For example, a skeet shell was designed to perform best when approaching an approximately thirty-inch circle from a distance of about forty yards.

EVOLUTION OF THE SHOTGUN

The ancient bell-mouth blunderbuss was the forerunner of the shotgun as we know it today. The fowling piece that followed it was a shorter, lighter version of the smooth bore musket. The flint-lock, on the other hand, which was slow to ignite, was used mostly for non-moving birds. Gunners found that a smooth bore musket loaded with a charge of shot pellets, produced results when used on sitting ducks, but was almost totally useless against birds on the wing. Consequently, wing shooting did not become popular until the advent of the percussion cap, with its more rapid ignition.

As the rifled barrel replaced the smooth bore musket, it became obvious that pellets used in bird shooting were unsuited for the rifled barrel. As a result, the shortened smooth-bore musket developed into a fowling piece or shotgun. Early shotguns were made with both single and double barrels and soon acquired the basic characteristics of today's shotgun. Although in use earlier, the breech-loading shotgun did not come into common use until about 1880, when the modern shotshell appeared.

CHOKE

Soon after the breech-loading shotgun appeared, choke boring was invented. It was discovered that by contricting ("choking") the bore at the muzzle, a narrower, denser pattern of shot was thrown, thereby extending the gun's

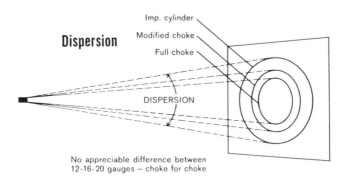

Dispersion

Imp. cylinder
Modified choke
Full choke

DISPERSION

No appreciable difference between
12-16-20 gauges — choke for choke

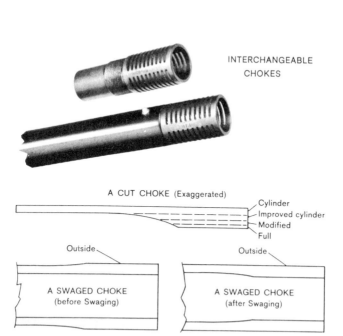

INTERCHANGEABLE
CHOKES

A CUT CHOKE (Exaggerated)

Cylinder
Improved cylinder
Modified
Full

Outside

Outside

A SWAGED CHOKE
(before Swaging)

A SWAGED CHOKE
(after Swaging)

effective range. The shotguns most commonly used in trapshooting today have a full choke. On the other hand, since skeet targets are at closer range and usually not going away as they are in trap, skeet guns have barrels that are not choked or constricted at the muzzle. They are called "open choke," or "true cylinder," or "cylinder bore" guns.

There are several degrees of choke: full choke; improved modified; modified choke; and improved cylinder or cylinder bore. *Full choke* barrels are designed for long range shooting; they tend to make the shot-pattern more dense at longer distances. *Improved modified choke* falls between full choke and modified choke; it is not commonly used in either trap or skeet shooting. *Modified choke* is a compromise between full choke and improved cylinder. Some gunners, when shooting doubles trap or modified clay pigeon events, prefer to have one barrel with a modified choke (for the first shot) and the other with full choke (for the second shot). *Improved cylinder*, or *cylinder bore* barrels, have little if any constriction and give maximum controlled spread of the shot charge for close shooting, as in skeet. *Open choke* and skeet choke are synonymous with cylinder bore.

SHOT PATTERNS

Shot patterns are closely associated with choke. The amount of choke effects the spread or pattern of the shot. Patterns at forty yards are used as a standard measure. Patterning a shotgun means shooting at a stationary target that will keep the marks of the shot hitting it. This can be done by shooting at a large paper target. Sometimes it is done by shooting at a large steel plate that has been coated with white lead or some similar substance. White lead is thick, dries very slowly and will record the mark of each pellet as it strikes the plate.

Each shotgun delivers a different pattern and the pattern changes with each load. The pellet marks on the paper will denote whether the gun is shooting where the shooter is looking and whether the gun fits the shooter. A shotgun should be patterned before each season's use, but certainly after any alterations have been made on it.

130

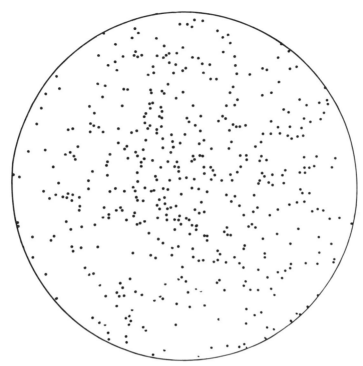

Shot pattern, Skeet: 12 gauge—3 drams—1⅛ ounces No. 9 shot; 30-inch circle. At 25 yards average pattern 62–67%.

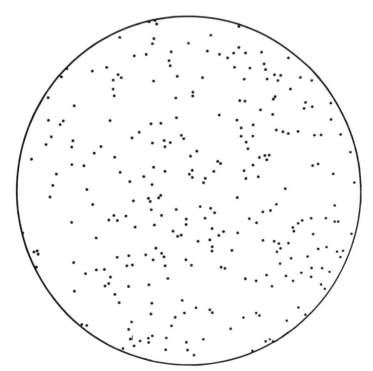

Shot Pattern, Skeet: 12 gauge—3 drams—1⅛ ounces No. 9 shot; 30-inch circle. At 35 yards average pattern 40–45%.

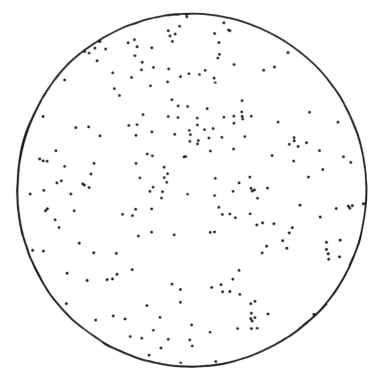

Shot Pattern, Skeet: 12 gauge—3 drams—1⅛ ounces No. 9 shot; 30-inch circle. At 40 yards average pattern 35–40%.

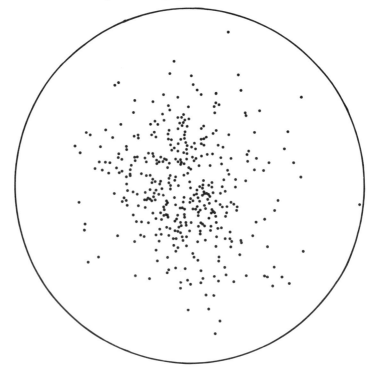

Shot Pattern, Trap: 12 gauge—3 drams—1⅛ ounces No. 7½ shot; 30-inch circle. Full choke at 25 yards average pattern 100%.

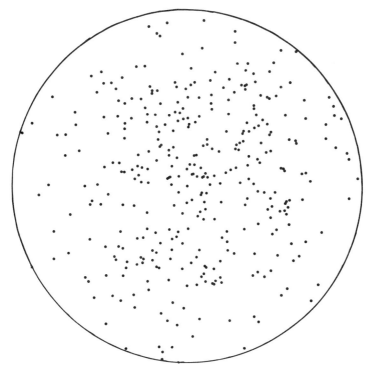

Shot Pattern, Trap: 12 gauge—3 drams—1⅛ ounces No. 7½ shot; 30-inch circle. Full choke at 35 yards average pattern 80–85%.

HOW TO PATTERN A SHOTGUN

Set the large cardboard or piece of paper forty yards from the shooting point. A black bull's eye on the paper is used as an aiming point. After firing, the target is inspected and a circle thirty inches in diameter is drawn to include the greatest number of pellet holes. Disregard the bull's eye; it may or may not be in the center of the drawn circle After counting the holes in the circle the number is compared to the number of shot known to be in identical shot shells having the same shot size and weight of shot.

Chokes of particular constrictions will produce the following results in a thirty-inch circle at forty yards:

Full Choke: 65-75% of charge
Improved Modified Choke: 55-65%
Modified Choke: 45-55%
Improved Cylinder Choke: 35-45%
Cylinder Bore: 25-35%

Chokes that are an integral part of the gun are made either by cutting or by swaging. Cut chokes are formed by reaming the barrel, with the reaming tool carrying the shape, radius, and dimensions of the choke desired. Swaged chokes are first formed on the barrel's exterior with less metal ground from the muzzle end than from the rest of the barrel. When the muzzle is swaged in a heavy press the excess metal on the exterior of the muzzle is pressed inward, creating an interior constriction of the desired shape and dimension.

Patterning A Shotgun

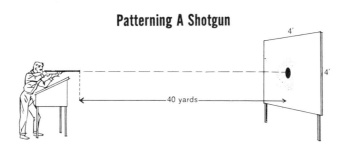

Checking the Patterns

Aiming point

Pencil

15″

String

1″ right

1″ low

Center of 30″ circle
containing most shot holes

Checking the Pattern. In this case gun shoots 1″ to right and 1″ low at 40 yards. If the shot holes inside the 30″ circle—drawn to include maximum number of shot holes—add up to 70% of pellets in a full load, gun is shooting a full choke pattern. Patterns will vary from shot to shot—several patterns should be fired and an average taken.

Several adjustable chokes are marketed, and interchangeable chokes that screw into a threaded muzzle are also available. But these are not often seen at trap and skeet fields. Both types are sometimes coupled with recoil-reducing attachments called compensators, which allow powder gases to escape sideways from vents at the muzzle. The compensator devices may reduce recoil to some extent, but the report is magnified—and that does not go over well at trap and skeet fields.

GAUGE

The term "gauge," as it refers to guns and shells, is an archaic one. It derives from the number of round lead balls needed to make a pound. For example, a 12-gauge gun had a bore which, if it had no choke, would accept one round ball, twelve of which would weigh a pound. Although this outmoded means of measurement is no longer applied in marketing practice, it has remained in use. Actually, because of the gun's choke, solid balls for a 12-gauge gun weigh only one ounce, or sixteen to the pound. Incidentally, the term "bore," synonymous with gauge, is used mostly by British gunners.

In using gauge as an indication of measurement, the smaller the number, the bigger the gauge. In other words, 12-gauge guns have larger diameter barrels than 16-gauge guns, 16's are larger than 20's, etc. There is one exception: the .410 bore refers to the actual barrel diameter, .410 inch; being a relatively latecomer to the shotgun group, it got by the older nomenclature. Because the bore is larger, the 12-gauge can handle more shot than the 16, and so on.

BARRELS

Modern shotguns are equipped with 26-, 28-, 30-, and 32-inch barrels, in 12 gauge. Smaller gauges usually come in 26-inch and 28-inch lengths. There is a mistaken notion that the reason why trapshooting guns are longer than skeet guns is because they shoot harder, or they keep a denser pattern for a longer period of time, which is an advantage in trapshooting. This is not so. Let us back track a bit. A barrel has to be long enough to allow complete combustion of the powder. Generally, when the shot charge has moved about twenty inches of the barrel length, combustion has been completed (with smokeless powder as far as velocities are concerned); therefore, the trap gun's thirty-inch barrel has no advantage over a skeet gun's twenty-six-

SHOTGUN GAUGES

The approximate bore diameter of each shotgun gauge shown below is the result of the original method of determining gauge by counting the number of lead balls per pound for each gauge gun, except the 410 which is a caliber, not a gauge.

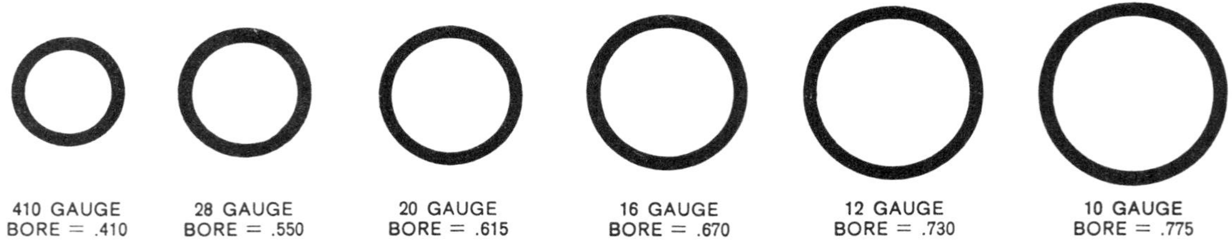

410 GAUGE
BORE = .410

28 GAUGE
BORE = .550

20 GAUGE
BORE = .615

16 GAUGE
BORE = .670

12 GAUGE
BORE = .730

10 GAUGE
BORE = .775

inch barrel. Length of barrel has little effect on velocity. Skeet barrels are shorter because shorter barrels make for faster gun-swinging at skeet targets. On the other hand, the trap barrel's longer length, with more weight out front, steadies the swing and favors a more accurate point and lead for the longer-range, and a more deliberate style of gun pointing, which is usually needed when firing at predominantly going-away targets.

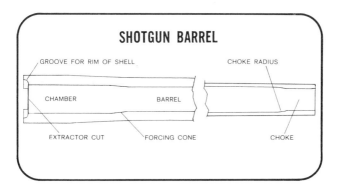

CHAMBER

The chamber, located at the breech end of all barrels, is larger in diameter than the barrel proper. The chamber houses the live shell and is longer than the shell so that the crimp can unfold when the shell is fired. Between the chamber and the barrel, the "cone," a funnel-like construction, narrows down from the end of the chamber to meet the barrel. The shell's rim falls into a groove at the rear of the chamber. The chamber also has a cut large enough to allow the extractor or ejector to be held under the shell rim.

Breech of a single barrel shotgun. The breech is the rear end of a firearm where the shell is inserted into the chamber.

The breech of a double barrel shotgun.

In the United States, most shotguns are chambered for 2¾-inch shells (12, 16, and 20 gauges). Some guns used for hunting, especially for duck hunting, have 3-inch chambers to accommodate 3-inch magnum loads for high flying birds in pass shooting. The .410 shotguns are also usually bored for 3-inch shells, because they are the most popular among .410 shooters.

Ventilated rib barrels are often specified for trap and skeet shooting. The open spaces between barrel and rib prevent any heat mirage caused by rapid firing.

VENTILATED RIB

The barrels of many modern shotguns, including trap and skeet guns, are fitted with ventilated ribs. The rib, supported by stanchions leaving an open space between the rib and barrel, serves two purposes. First, it is a straight-edge, so to speak, to assist in gun pointing and sighting down the barrel. Second, it breaks up the heat mirage that shimmers up from a barrel hot from continuous firing, which otherwise may confuse the gunner's view of his target.

SIGHTS

Sights on a shotgun are not as important as those on a rifle because the shooter *points* the gun at the moving target. In rifle shooting, the sights are

In correct sighting, the pupil of the eye acts as the rear sight; it should not be below or above the sighting plane of the barrel. The instructor can check this important fact by standing in front of the beginner's gun and looking directly down the top of the barrel to the eye. Needless to say, the instructor personally examines the chamber of the gun for shells, puts the safety on, and tells the learner not to place his finger on the trigger (as in the facing photograph).

One of the easiest ways to teach correct gun position is to have the beginner set the gun to shoulder and sight along the barrel. Then the left arm and hand are brought up to meet the gun. Without moving cheek from stock, head and arms are brought down to shooting posture. This method assures that the gun butt will rest properly high and in the hollow of the shoulder. Correct positioning of gun at shoulder is especially important for females.

In group teaching the instructor will find it helpful to have his students first follow targets by pointing at them with forefinger and arm fully extended. The target is followed, passed, and when proper lead has been attained the trigger is pulled. Note that after the trigger is pulled and the target hit, the gunner continues the swing or "follow through".

used for precise *aiming*. Shotgun sights are beads of various sizes and colors; one is just as good as another. They help prevent canting the gun, and also help in aligning the eye along the length of the barrel *before* the target is called for. In other words, if the gunner's eye is on the same level as the front bead but above the second or middle bead it will cause him to overshoot the target.

Actually, the rear sight of a shotgun is the eye of the shooter. For consistent shooting, the eye should be in the same position for every shot, looking directly down the center line and slightly above the receiver or rib, just high enough to see the target.

140

STOCK

Manufacturers produce guns that have stocks suitable for men of average build. About seventy percent of shooters can adapt themselves to these "on the rack" guns. Shooters of average physique, who find that they are consistently placing their aiming eye improperly, need to have special stocks made to suit them. For example, a tall person with long arms may need a ½- or ¾-of-an-inch spacer inserted between the butt of the gun and the recoil pad, thereby making the stock longer. In contrast, persons with arms shorter than average many need the stock shortened.

Special Stocks

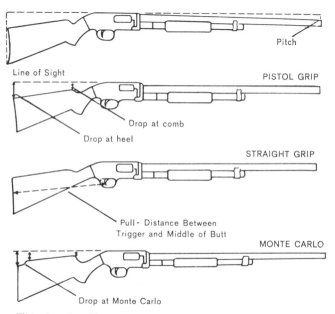

This drawing illustrates the measurements necessary in ordering a shotgun stock to the individual shooter's own measurements. The necessary measurements are: Drop at comb, drop at heel, length of pull, pitch and circumference of grip. For Monte Carlo stock add the drop at Monte Carlo.

Stocks that are too short usually cause improper mounting of the gun, resulting in shoulder ache because of recoil. Or the point of the comb may dig the cheek. Or the thumb may bump the nose. Stocks that have too much drop at the heel hurt the face because they have a tendency to push upwards

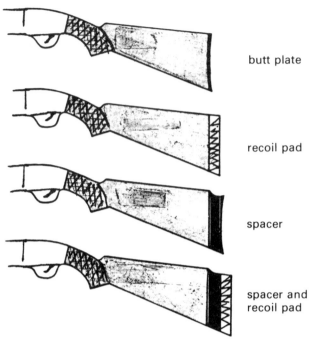

butt plate

recoil pad

spacer

spacer and
recoil pad

Butt Plate, Recoil Pad, Spacer, Spacer
and Recoil Pad. To change stock length
attach a recoil pad. If more length is required a spacer is added.

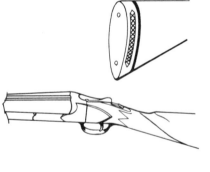

The recoil pad is a rubber cushion that
eases or softens the recoil against a
shooter's shoulder.

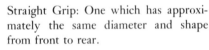

Straight Grip: One which has approximately the same diameter and shape
from front to rear.

Pistol Grip: One which swells out downward and to the rear in a form approxi-
mating the handle of a pistol.

more on recoil. Also, an excessive drop at the heel will not allow the entire butt to rest against the shoulder, causing a bruising recoil.

"Drops" are measured from a straight edge laid along the top of the muzzle and receiver, or along the rib if the gun has one. The comb is the top front of the stock; the heel is the top point of the butt. The distance from the straight edge to these points is the comb and heel drop. Stock length is measured from the front center of the trigger to the center end of the butt plate. Average shotgun stocks are provided with a 14-inch pull: that is, the distance from trigger to butt.

There is a major difference between the stock shapes of trap and skeet guns. Trap shots are fired at rising, going-away targets; therefore, trapshooters prefer stocks with a straighter comb over those with more drop.

For trap and skeet shooting, stocks should be equipped with a rubber recoil pad that eases recoil and helps prevent the gun butt from slipping from the shoulder pocket.

Shock absorbers can also be inserted inside the length of the stock. Any good gun-repair man is capable of adding the recoil pad, or shortening the stock, or inserting the internal shock absorber.

TYPES OF GUNS

The two most popular types of trap and skeet guns in use today are the semi-automatic and the over-and-under. Also in use, but far less popular,

There are two general classes of shotguns:

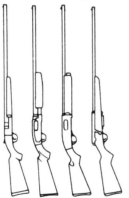
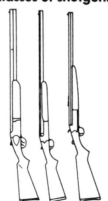

1. SINGLE BARREL GUNS
- Single shot
- Slide action or pump
- Auto loading
- Bolt action repeater

2. DOUBLE BARREL GUNS
- Over-and-under
- Side-by-side
- A combination of one smooth bore and one rifle barrel

143

are the double barrel and the slide action guns. The single shot is used as a "youth gun" and is an excellent gun to use when teaching youngsters. All of these guns are manufactured in all conventional gauges and chokes.

SEMI-AUTOMATICS

The semi-automatics are known as self-loaders, auto-loaders, or automatics. They are generally the most popular shotgun used in the clay target games because they are the least expensive and the recoil is not felt as sharply as it is with the other styles of guns. Although developed in America they are now being produced in Europe and Japan and are imported in considerable numbers.

The semi-automatics are gas-operated shotguns, which are activated by gas pressure tapped from the barrel. They operate on a piston that is hooked up to the action. After causing the action to open, the spent gas escapes through a gas port as the piston returns under spring pressure. The takedown system is simple. Barrels interchange without factory fitting. Although the modern semi-automatic is very reliable and works well with reloaded ammunition, it must be kept clean and not over-oiled. Most of the semi-automatic "hang-ups" or malfunctions that occur on the trap and skeet fields happen because the gun was not well cleaned or was over-oiled.

OVER-AND-UNDER

The over-and-under is one of the most reliable and safest of all shotguns because it has two single barrels or single-shots joined in the same frame. This gun offers the advantage of different chokes: an open barrel for the first shot and a more tightly choked barrel for the second. Skeet guns, however, usually contain open chokes in both barrels.

One of the plus factors in the over-and-under is the single sighting plane it provides along the top of the upper barrel. It can be lined up the same as a slide action or semi-automatic and gives the same "sight picture."

SLIDE ACTION

The slide action, commonly called "pump gun," is rarely seen on the skeet field, where doubles are involved. Not many shooters can pump a slide-action gun as fast as they can get off two shots with a semi-automatic or an over-and-under.

The pump gun has a movable fore-end, usually made of wood, to work the action. After firing the shell, it is pulled back towards the shooter and consequently opens the action and rejects the empty shell. The fore-end is shoved forward, and by this movement the action is closed and another shell is shoved into the chamber. The gun is then again ready for firing.

Pump guns can be single-loaded through the port and into the chamber, or the second shell (in skeet) can be slid into the magazine.

Loading an over-and-under shotgun.

Loading an auto-loader shotgun. The first shell is inserted and the breech closed before the second shell is placed in the magazine.

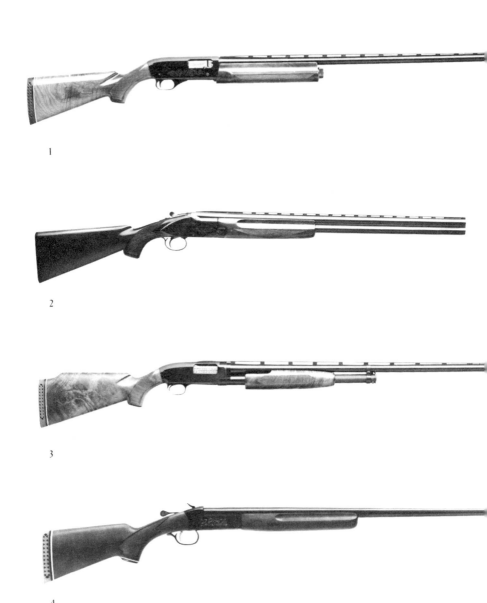

The auto-loader (1) and the over-and-under (2) are the most popular types of shotguns used today on trap and skeet fields. The slide action (3) with the Monte Carlo stock remains a popular choice with many trapshooters. The single barrel (4) is an excellent firearm to use in teaching youngsters how to shoot.

146

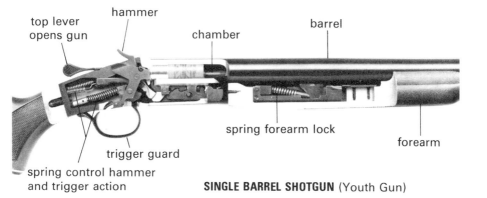

SINGLE BARREL SHOTGUN (Youth Gun)

In shooting American trap the pump gun is not a liability since only one shot has to be fired at a time and the speed of pumping the action is not crucial.

DOUBLE BARREL

The double barrel, or side-by-side, has lost popularity as a trap and skeet gun, but it is still regarded by many as the "classic" shotgun, not for clay target shooting but for upland game hunting. Most experts consider a well balanced double to be the finest of all guns to handle. A good double, how-

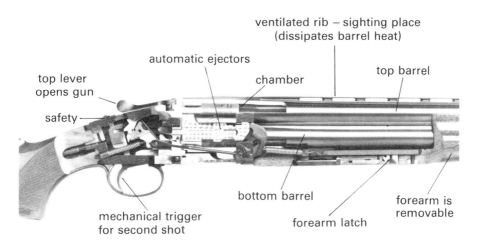

OVER-AND-UNDER SHOTGUN

147

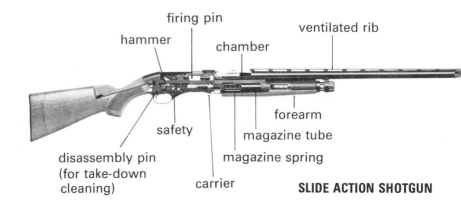

firing pin

hammer

ventilated rib

chamber

forearm

safety

magazine tube

disassembly pin
(for take-down
cleaning)

magazine spring

carrier

SLIDE ACTION SHOTGUN

SEMI-AUTOMATIC or AUTOLOADER

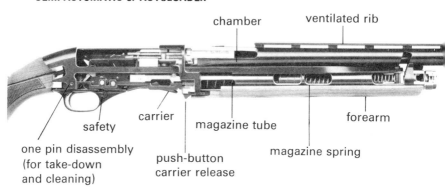

chamber

ventilated rib

carrier

forearm

safety

magazine tube

one pin disassembly
(for take-down
and cleaning)

push-button
carrier release

magazine spring

ever, is very expensive, which is one of the reasons why few appear on trap and skeet fields.

Like the over-and-under, the side-by-side provides the advantage of two quick shots from differently choked barrels. Some double guns have two triggers, one for each barrel. The better grades have single triggers which can be quickly set to fire either barrel first, plus automatic ejectors that pop one, or both, fired shells when the gun is opened.

SINGLE-SHOT

Single-shot shotguns are not commonly seen on the trap field because the good ones are very expensive. They are usually superbly constructed and choked to a degree of full choke sometimes known as "super pucker" or

148

"really full." These highly choked barrels produce a tight cluster of shot, which is perfect for handicap shooters who often hit targets at distances of fifty to sixty yards.

On the other hand, there are single barrel shotguns manufactured in the United States that are the least expensive of all shotguns. The single-shots are the break-open, down-swinging-barrel type. Some have top levers, some have side levers, and a few models are worked by a bottom lever. They are all rugged and about as safe as a shot gun can be.

The single-shot in 20 gauge is an excellent gun to use when teaching youngsters to shoot at clay targets. One of its best features pertains to safety. The instructor can cock the gun by pulling back the hammer only when the gun is shouldered by the beginner and ready to shoot.

GUN CARE

Improved ammunition, with non-corrosive primers and an all-plastic wad, has greatly changed gun care in the past twenty-five years. The plastic wad scrubs the barrel out each time the gun is fired, thereby eliminating the need to clean the barrel after each shoot. Scrubbing the barrel with a wire brush (with the thought that an extra clean barrel will help the pellets form a better pattern) is not necessary.

If the gun has been used in rainy or damp weather, an oily rag run through the barrel is all the scrubbing required. Since wet shells will leave dampness in the chamber, light oil should be sprayed into the chamber to prevent rusting. And, all the exterior metal parts of the gun should be wiped with a dry cloth. Always allow your shotgun to adjust to room temperature before applying oil. Then wipe again with an oily rag. Aerosol lubricants that contain a desiccant or moisture-replacing agent may also be used. The oil, of course, should be light gun oil. A very light spray of WD40 or similar product with the excess wiped off will do the job. Also, all oil should be wiped off completely the next time the gun is used. After oiling the outside of the gun, the metal should not be touched; hold it by the stock or forearm. If the metal is handled, fingerprints will be imprinted and the salt of the hand and fingers will cause rusting if left long enough.

The double guns—over-and-under and the side-by-side—require very little inside cleaning. A drop of oil on the extractors, on the area where the barrel hinges on the receiver, and on the action release on top of the receiver, is all the oiling required to keep the gun in good working order.

The slide action or pump gun must be given more care in oiling. The major flaw in oiling a pump gun is too much oil. A receiver full of oil will drastically retard the action. Perhaps once, or twice if the gun is heavily used, remove the trigger guard and pop in a drop or two of thin oil on the trigger mechanism. If it is necessary to remove dirt, use a stiff paint brush to wash the assembly in gasoline and allow to dry before applying the oil.

The semi-automatics, the most popular of the trap and skeet guns, require special attention if they are to perform well. The auto-loaders give most trouble if not cleaned because they have the greatest number of moving parts. The gas system, immediately beneath the fore-end, is the most important area requiring regular cleaning. Powder residue builds up gradually on the magazine tube along which the gas piston and action bar sleeve slide. If not cleaned for some time and over many rounds of shooting, this residue will mount up to retard the movement of the auto-loading action and result in a malfunctioning gun. If a dirty gas system is the main reason for performance problems with the semi-automatics, the second reason is an over-lubricated gas system.

All auto-loaders should be cleaned after a day's shooting, if 100 rounds or more were fired, or if 100 to 200 rounds were put through the gun since its last cleaning. Cleaning the gas system will prevent residue build-up and assure a smooth functioning gun.

It is not a great chore to clean the piston rings, magazine tube and action bar assembly; the task requires but a few minutes. They should be wiped off with fine steel wool and a clean rag. No oil is necessary. Also, the gas parts in the barrel ring should be inspected to be sure they are not clogged with burned powder. Depending upon the amount of use the gun gets, it should be field-stripped occasionally. The trigger assembly and receiver should be cleaned with gasoline. After allowing them time to dry, a little spray of fine oil should be applied to all moving parts. Some auto-loaders require extra cleaning of the gas cap. Some shooters carry an extra cap to replace the dirty one. Then they clean the one removed when they get home.

Before storing a gun for any length of time, a thorough cleaning and oiling are required. (Again, be careful not to handle the metal portions of the gun once it has been oiled.)

The shotgun should not be stored for a long period in a leather or plastic gun case, especially the type that is lined with cloth, fleece or other material. The lining either rubs off or absorbs some of the oil, thereby exposing the metal to rust in spots. If a gun must be stored in such a manner, it should be inspected once a month to check for signs of rust. Store the gun in a conventional wooden gun case, if possible. Some shooters have a special rack situated in a "gun closet" behind a false wall that appears to be part of the room wall. An arrangement of this type makes the guns invisible in case a thief breaks into the house. The gun rack includes a metal bar that is locked into place in order to keep children from tampering with the guns. It is hardly necessary to mention that guns should never be stored away loaded. If children are in the house, or if unpredictable adults are in the household, the ammunition should never be stored in the same spot as the guns. Ammunition is easier to hide than shotguns, and that should be done if there is the slightest possibility of unauthorized hands getting into guns and ammo.

When transporting a shotgun, not only should it be unloaded, it should be broken down and carried in a case. If you are traveling a short distance, such as to the gun club, leather or plastic cases are acceptable. However, the trunk type case lined with plastic cushions is by far superior. Such a case protects the gun from being damaged in the trunk of the car. Also, the short gun case, where the gun must be broken down before recasing it, reminds the shooter that it should be cleaned. When using the standard, full-length, zippered case there is a tendency for the gunner to shove the gun into the case and forget it.

When travelling by train or by air, the shallow, hard, trunk-like case is a must. If the gun is carried in a full-length leather case, everyone knows it is a gun, but few people realize that the long, box-like case holds a firearm and less eyebrows are raised.

Anyone who has travelled by air realizes that baggage takes a beating. Although the modern gun case is made of tough plastic with reinforced corners, there is always a possibility that the locks may be tampered with or hit accidentally causing the case to open. As a precaution, any gun that is meant to travel by air as personal baggage should be strapped completely around the case in two areas. The best strapping material is insulating tape, which is available in most hardware stores. It really sticks, and it is unusually strong.

Usually, the airlines require only that the gunner advise the personnel at the check-in station that the case contains a gun. No ammunition is allowed to be placed in with the gun. Some airlines allow a maximum of five pounds of ammo to be carried in a suitcase checked as baggage. Usually, one gun is allowed per person. Before even bringing the gun to the airport, however, the shooter should personally check with his airline for specific information about rules regarding guns as baggage.

When the Yale Trap and Skeet teams travel by car I give them the following instructions:

1. The guns must be unloaded, broken down, and the barrels of the semi-automatic removed.
2. Place the guns in hard cases and lock them.
3. Set the cases in the trunk or the luggage compartment (someone should carry an extra set of keys). The cases should be on the bottom, covered by other luggage.
4. If it is an overnight trip, the guns must be taken into the motel rooms, and before dark.
5. If, by chance, you have to prove to the motel management or anyone else that, in fact, the guns are for recreational shooting, someone in the

group (usually I as coach) should have a copy of the shoot's intended program.

6. When travelling with guns, never exceed the speed limit. If stopped for speeding, or any other traffic violation, the police officer may look through the car, and if he finds ammo or guns he may, at best, restrain the group for enough time to make the team late for the shoot. And worst of all, it is possible that the guns could be taken and held by the police, depending upon the area of travel. As an example, I tell the team never to travel through New York City or Boston, where the car may well be stopped by a policeman for a minor reason, such as slowing down because of confused travel directions. It is entirely possible, in such a case, to fall into the hands of a local policeman who doesn't know a skeet gun from a bazooka—and that could mean big trouble.

FITTING THE SHOTGUN

A shotgun is correctly fitted when the gunner feels comfortable shooting it, when no part of the gun interferes with the shooter's sighting or swinging. There is no doubt that when a shotgun that *truly* fits, the shooter's accuracy will be at least thirty percent higher than with an ill-fitting gun.

In Europe, gun-fitting is done with much more concern and fanfare than it is in the United States. There, it is generally only the more affluent who participate in bird hunting and the clay target games, and they invariably purchase their guns from old, famous gun companies that produce a relatively small number of firearms annually. These companies have very capable gun fitters who tailor the guns exactly to the purchaser's physical build. American gunners who can afford it travel to England, for example, to order shotguns that will be specifically designed to fit them. Such custom fitting is often done with a *try-gun*, first used by such fine English gunmakers as Purdey and Holland and Holland. The try-gun is a gun with an adjustable stock. The customer seats the gun to his shoulder and the expert then adjusts the length of the try-stock, extending the butt plate attached to bars that can slide in or out of the stock. Also, the mechanism that connects the stock to the gun proper can be raised or lowered. When both the expert and the purchaser are satisfied with the fit, an order is drawn up for a custom-built stock.

In America, where guns are produced in great volume, and sold at reasonable cost, manufacturers have arrived at a formula for making guns that will fit about seventy percent of the people buying them. Some of the remaining thirty percent will adapt themselves to a gun that doesn't fit very well, although they shoot under a handicap. This is like a hiker wearing a tight pair of boots; he will get to his destination, but his heels will be blistered. Shooters who use ill-fitting guns never shoot well.

Although true gun fitting is a complex matter, a general "rule of thumb" calls for the first joint of the finger to reach the trigger comfortably while the butt of the gun rests in the crook of the elbow, as Tom Migdalski demonstrates.

The butt of the gun is not distributed evenly in the hollow of the shoulder. The toe of stock concentrates the recoil of the gun. Result: a bruised shoulder.

Head is brought down to the stock instead of bringing stock up to the head. This condition causes undershooting of targets.

154

Gun butt too high and out of the shoulder pocket causing pain to deltoid muscle on which it rests.

Extremely poor arm positions for trap and skeet shooting. This posture is typically one used by persons who have done some rifle shooting. Rigid arms and low elbows restrict smooth swing and follow through.

Arms and elbows that are over-extended upward cause fatigue.

Arm lowered to expose proper gun fit into shoulder. Tom has removed his shirt to demonstrate that when the gun is correctly shouldered the entire butt of the gun is solidly against shoulder, thereby spreading recoil that is more comfortable to absorb.

Examples of excellent form.

The balance is literally that point between butt and muzzle where a gun balances when rested on a fulcrum. However, this is not the popular understanding of the term. Neither is it an entirely popular understanding that a gun balances properly when the point of balance is midway between the points where the hands naturally hold it in shooting. In most cases, balance is understood to mean the feel it gives to the shooter in handling the gun—that is, whether correctly balanced or either muzzle light or muzzle heavy.

The stock is the major factor to consider in gun fit. If it is too short the gunner will lower his head to cheek the stock. This puts the eyes in the wrong relationship to the barrel. If the gunner sights too high along the barrel he will shoot over the target; if too low, he will shoot low. When the head is lowered to the stock it is also tilted, placing the eye at an angle to the barrel, which causes the shot charge to fly either to the right or left of the target. If the stock is very short for him, the shooter may receive an unpleasant jolt from the thumb hitting the nose. If the stock is too long, the beginner invariably holds his head too high. And stretching the trigger hand forward may cause the shooter's face to leave the stock.

Often, short and tall gunners shoot with these handicaps because they do not know the difference. Every gunner should take the time to analyse his particular gun-fit problems. One of the basic ways of discovering whether your gun has the proper length of pull (distance between center of trigger and center of butt plate) is to place the butt of the gun in the crook of the elbow. If the first joint of the trigger finger reaches the trigger comfortably, the stock is the correct length. If the first joint of the finger goes beyond the trigger, the gun may be a quarter to a half-inch too short. If the finger joint does not reach the trigger, the stock is too long. When a true gun fit is sought, however, the gunner must also take into account length of neck, length of arms, high or low cheek bones, etc.

Another test of gun fit can be tried. Hold the unloaded gun in the "off-shoulder" position. Then, with eyes closed, place the gun in shooting position with the butt cradled in your shoulder. Then open your eyes. If the gun fits, your eye should be sighting down the top of the barrel in perfect shooting position.

Of course, the easiest procedure in checking for gun fit is to visit a competent gunsmith, who will diagnose your fit. If the stock is short he will add a recoil pad (or a spacer if your gun already has a pad). If the gun is too long he will know how to cut the stock professionally. A stock that bruises the cheek may be too high at the comb, and can be corrected by removing some wood from the comb. The stock can be made straighter, if necessary, by rasping wood from the peak of the comb down to nothing at the heel. If that is insufficient, the stock is removed and the tang (rod that connects the gun to the stock) is secured in a vise and bent upward.

The measurement of the comb in relation to the rest of the shotgun is extremely important, because it determines the position of the eye (the eye itself acting as the gun's rear sight). For each shot, the eye must be positioned centrally over and only slightly above the rib or receiver groove. In other words, the gunner sees a flat, even surface as he sights down the barrel at the target.

It is easy to check your gun for correct drop at the comb. With the gun unloaded, open the breech, put the safety on, and mount the gun to your shoulder, being sure that the butt is secured in the hollow of the shoulder. Next, have your gun buddy stand directly in front of you. With your cheek on the comb and your nose about an inch from the base of your thumb, point the gun barrel at his eye. If he sees the pupil of your eye just as if it were resting on the back of the rib or receiver, the comb of the gun is perfect. If there is considerable space between the rib and the pupil, more drop at the comb is needed to lower the eye to correct position. If the eye is partially or completely hidden, less drop is needed. This problem is easy to correct. Simply add a comb pad, available at any good gun shop, to the comb. Pads come in ⅛-inch, ¼-inch, and ⅜-inch thicknesses. Another method is to add "moleskin" (a felt adhesive available in drug stores) to the comb until the necessary height is achieved.

Some gunners make these modifications themselves, cutting down the stock, adding a recoil pad, rasping the joint of the comb, and bending the tang. However, I advise any shooter who is not an accomplished mechanic to let a good gunsmith do the job.

16 - Shells

In England, shotgun shells are termed cartridges, but in the United States the term shotshells is so widely used it is now official. So shotgun shells are now referred to as "shells," and "cartridges" generally pertain to loaded rifle or pistol ammunition.

THE OLD SHELL

About a hundred years ago the shotshell came into being in a form resembling today's shell. For most of those years the shotshell tube was made from tightly wound paper set in a brass head. The inside of the head was

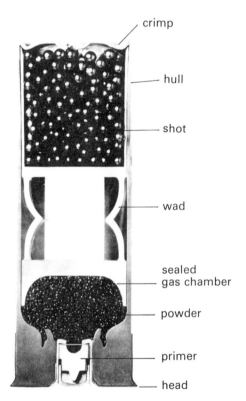

crimp

hull

shot

wad

sealed
gas chamber

powder

primer

head

A SHOT SHELL AND ITS COMPONENTS

reinforced with a base wad of treated cardboard, and a center fire primer was set in the rear or head of the brass exterior. Powder was poured over the base wad, and overpowder and filler wads of different sizes were set over the powder. The shot was poured into a tube and kept there by a cardboard top wad. The edges of the tube were then rolled down into a lip on the top wad.

Although the design of the modern shell remains basically the same as the shell of years past, it is far superior to its predecessor, due to the great advancement of shotgun technology in recent years. The tube or hull is now made of plastic; the lead shot or pellets are enclosed in a plastic wad; the primer contains a non-corrosive priming mixture; and the brass head is tougher.

THE HULL

One of the greatest improvements in the construction of the shotgun shell occurred when the plastic hull or tube was invented. Because plastic is tough and will not swell under damp conditions, as paper shells did, plastic hulls became an immediate favorite with trap and skeet shooters who load their own shells. Plastic shells have other advantages. Their ballistic stability is superior to that of paper shells, because plastic eliminates the effects of changing temperature on powder. Plastic shells slide easier into the gun chambers, an important feature when used in autoloaders.

In the 1940's, the plastic hull was also responsible for an important improvement in the wad structure of the shell. The cardboard top wads, more often than not, mingled with the shot as it left the gun barrel, disrupting the shot pattern. Now, instead of a top wad and the rolled-down edge of the tube being used to secure the load, the new tube's edge was simply crimped or folded down. The new system eliminated the top wad. Now when the shell is fired the crimps open up and the charge goes flying out without interference.

LEAD SHOT

Shotgun shells are offered in a variety of shot sizes, the size depending upon the clay target activity or the type of game the hunter is pursuing. Here we are concerned only with the ammunition used in the clay target games.

Although steel shot is gradually replacing lead shot in duck hunting loads, lead continues to be used in trap and skeet shells. Ballistically, lead is far superior to steel as a load in target shells, and it is much less expensive. One of the reasons why lead shot costs less than steel shot is because it is

Through this perforated dropping pan flows molten metal destined to become pellets for shot shells. After flowing through the bowl, the individual pellets form spherical shapes and drop 154 feet into a pool of water.

Molten lead droplets begin their fall inside a steel tube to a water bath at the tube base, which cushions the drop. This operation is the first step in the manufacture of lead shot for shot shells.

simpler to produce. Today, practically the same methods are employed in making lead pellets as were used when shotgun shells were first invented. Molten lead, when passed through a sieve-like device and dropped from a height, breaks into a spray of drops. Water, when dropped through a sieve from an equal height takes on a tear-shaped form. But lead emerges in near-perfect spheres.

The use of "shot towers" in the process of making lead pellets remains, in principle, the same as it was in colonial days. Metal pigs of alloys of lead, containing antimony and other hardening agents, are placed in elevators and transported to the top of the tower where they are melted. The lead is then poured into pan-shaped, sieve-like containers and strained, so to speak. The size of the holes on the bottom of the pan determines the size of the shot. The molten lead drops almost two hundred feet from the pans into a tank of water. The lead becomes round almost immediately after leaving the pan. The water is not used to chill the shot, as is popularly thought, but simply cushions its fall. Next, the shot is dried and brought to the tower again, and polished in a tumbling process. Then the pellets go through a culling device,

163

The dropping pan through which molten lead pours to eventually become pellets for shot shells. The number of holes in a pan varies with the size of shot being made.

STANDARD SHOT CHART — Diameter in inches

No.	12	11	10	9	8	7½	6	5	4	2
	.05	.06	.07	.08	.09	.095	.11	.12	.13	.15

APPROXIMATE NUMBER OF PELLETS TO THE OUNCE									
2385	1380	870	585	410	350	225	170	135	90

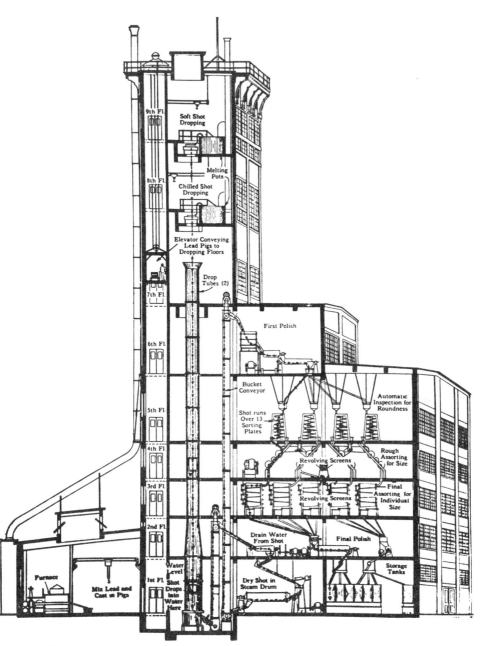

A traditional method of making lead shot: the shot tower, nine floors high, with its associated facilities. After molten lead droplets fall into the pool of water that cushions their fall, the irregular pellets are culled, the shot is assorted for size, polished, and stored in tanks.

travelling down a series of inclined planes. The out-of-round pellets fall into a trough and are returned to be remelted and reprocessed.

Many attempts have been made to improve on this old fashioned way of making shot pellets, but as yet, no method has been found to be as efficient as the drop-tower operation.

The standard loads for 12-gauge trap and skeet shells contain 1⅛ ounces of shot. The 20-gauge skeet shell holds ⅞ ounce; 28 gauge, ¾ ounce; and the .410 has ½ ounce. Shells used for hunting contain heavier loads of lead pellets. For example 12-gauge magnum shells may have 1¼, 1½, or as much as 1⅞ ounces of shot.

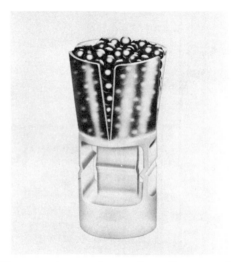

The one piece wad provides pellet protection, minimizes recoil through a cushionary device, and maintains a positive gas seal over powder for better patterning.

THE WAD

One major defect of shotgun shells, recognized by manufacturers for many years, was the abrasive action of the gun barrel upon the outer ring of pellets as they were fired out. In exiting, they rubbed against the walls of the barrel and became flattened, consequently affecting the shot pattern, often causing it to fly wide of the mark. Technicians tried wrapping the pellets in various ways in order to protect the shot as it travelled down the bore, but none were satisfactory until manufacturers developed a method of using a thin strip of plastic in which to wrap the shot charge. The next improvement was a self-contained plastic wad and shot protector, with the rear end formed

166

in an upside down, cup-like pattern that creates a gas-sealed chamber when the powder is ignited. The middle of the plastic wad progressively collapses at ignition, and absorbs shock that helps prevent pellet deformation.

POWDER

The powder, when ignited by the primer, burns rapidly, forming gases which, in expanding, propel the shot out of the barrel. One of the great improvements in construction of the shotgun shells was the replacement of black powder with smokeless powder.

The shells used in 12-gauge American trap and skeet events contain either 2¾ or 3 "drams equivalent" of powder. The term "drams equiv." printed on boxes of shells refers to the unit of measurement used in the early days of shotgunning to designate the amount of black powder in the charge (the avoirdupois dram being equal to $1/16$ of an ounce). When the first smokeless powders came into use they were made to load in a volume equal to that of black powder. For example, three drams of smokeless powder had about the same ballistic capabilities as three drams of black powder. As smokeless powder continued to be improved, however, the volume-for-volume concept ceased to be valid. Nevertheless, the original terminology was retained, since gunners were familiar with it. Consequently, manufacturers still designate the smokeless powder loads as equivalent to black-powder drams, even though the smokeless powders now represent only a part of that weight.

Some shooters prefer the 3 drams equiv. when participating in handicap trap, modified clay pigeon, and international skeet. Shells used for hunting hold larger amounts of powder. Magnums may contain 4½ drams equiv.

PRIMER

The primer is a small metal cap that fits into the center of the brass head. It contains a sensitive explosive compound which, when struck by the firing pin, ignites the powder. It was in the 1920's that a non-corrosive priming mixture was introduced. It eliminated the need for gun cleaning after each firing.

THE BASIC SHELL CATEGORIES

There are two basic categories of shotgun shells: those used in trap, skeet, and the other clay target games, and those used in the field for hunting, including long range and magnum shells. A variety of powder and shot-size

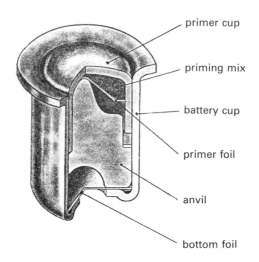

primer cup

priming mix

battery cup

primer foil

anvil

bottom foil

SHOT SHELL BATTERY CUP PRIMER

combinations, as well as gauges, are available in each category. The brass bases of 12- and 20-gauge trap and skeet shells are low in comparison to the bases of long-range and magnum shells. The shells used in clay-target shooting create lower internal pressures on ignition than do long-range loads; therefore, they do not require as much metal as the high-base hunting shells to contain these pressures. Low base shells in 12, 16, and 20 gauges are generally used in hunting small upland game and birds. The 28 and .410 gauge target shells are high base. The standard length of both high and low base shells in 12, 16, 20 and 28 gauges in 2¾ inches. In 10 gauge, standard shells are available in 2¾ and 2⅞ inches. The .410 gauge guns are nearly all chambered to accommodate the 3-inch shells, but they will take the 2½-inch ones as well.

Magnum shells are available in both 2¾- and 3-inch lengths. These shells are never used in clay target shooting; they provide extra power for hitting game at long ranges.

Rifled slugs and buckshot shells, of course, are not used in flying-target shooting. The rifled slug used in deer hunting is a solid cylindrical lead projectile with rifling grooves gauged into its outside face. The grooves cause the slug to spin when fired from the smooth bore of a shotgun.

A buckshot load, also used for hunting, contains a group of large lead pellets, much fewer but much bigger than those found in standard shot sizes.

168

TRACER SHELLS

Another type of shot shell, used mostly to correct trap and skeet shooting faults, is the "tracer shell." These tracer loads vividly show, under all light conditions, the actual path of the shot column, and they eliminate any doubts as to why a target was missed.

A word of caution: the tracer shells contain a flammable substance and are for use only in areas where there is no possibility of the tracer igniting flammable material on impact. A distance of at least one hundred yards should be allowed for the tracer to burn out.

PROOF SHELLS

"Proof shells" are especially produced for use by firearms manufacturers to test the strength of a gun's chamber, barrel, and action. These shells are loaded with much heavier charges of powder than any clay target or hunting ammunition. Manufacturers use proof shells to check out the quality and safety of a gun by firing one or more of these potent shells. All proof firing is done under rigidly controlled and supervised conditions. Such testing proves that the gun is safe for use with commercial ammunition. In the United States, the manufacturer proofs the guns and affixes a "proof mark" (a symbol or letter) to the gun. In some countries, the proofing is supervised by government inspectors and the gun is stamped accordingly.

Proof shells are conspicuously marked and loaded into hulls of atypical coloration. However, the danger lies in the fact that some shotgunners, who make a hobby of collecting shotgun shells, include live proof shells in their collection. A proof shell, fired by mistake in a trap or skeet gun, could be disastrous.

Manufacturers continue to develop "specialty" shells for different types of shooting, not only for various kinds of game in hunting, but also for the clay target games—handicap trap, modified clay pigeon, and international skeet. The shells used in skeet must comply with the standards of shot and powder set by the NSSA. Those used in trap are guided by the rules of the ATA. Modified clay pigeon rules regarding shooting and ammunition are controlled by the NRA. The rules pertaining to shot and powder used in international events are to be found in the International Shooting Union's book of rules. (NRA is the U.S. affiliate.)

17 - Targets

SIZE AND COMPOSITION

Today's standard target has a diameter of 4¼ inches; its total height is 1¹/₁₆ inches; and its weight is 3½ ounces. Composed basically of asphalt pitch and ground lime, it has to be strong enough to withstand the shock of being heaved out at a high rate of speed by the arm of the target-throwing machine, yet fragile enough to break when hit by a few No. 9 pellets at thirty or forty yards.

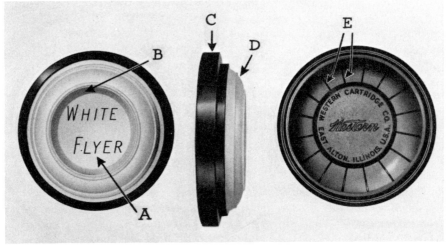

The Standard Target has a diameter of 4¼ inches; total height is 1¹/₁₆ inches; weight is 3½ ounces. It is basically composed of asphalt pitch and ground lime. Targets are available with domes of different colors. A—Poker Chip; B—Ledge; C—Flange; D—Dome; E—Scorings.

COST

Clay targets are not expensive. They are packaged 135 to the case. A squad of five shooters needs a minimum of 125 targets for a round of skeet or American trap. The extra ten birds are usually consumed in the same round;

some are thrown for the initial viewing by the squad, others serve as replacements for any targets that are broken when they come flying out of the house, or for repeating premature or late pulls.

COLOR

The color of the target dome varies, depending upon the surrounding environment of the shooting fields and the preference of management and shooters. Originally, white dome targets were mostly used, then yellow became popular; then orange domes came in, and the latest rage is for fluorescent orange and fluorescent green; they seem to flash on dark or overcast days, in early morning and at dusk. Many shooters claim that these targets are the easiest to see.

WHERE AND HOW TO BUY

Clay targets can be bought by the case in most stores that sell guns and ammunition, but they are also available in carload lots. Many clubs buy them this way because money can be saved and the fees per round to club members can be lowered. However, it requires a group of volunteers to unload the huge trailer truck. Also a large weather proof storage area must be available, though not necessarily at the shooting grounds. An occasional trip to the storehouse with a station wagon or a pickup truck is all that is necessary to keep up the field's supply of targets.

STORING

The lower section of the high house on the skeet field is used for storing cases of targets so that they are easily accessible if needed for a big shoot. Extra cases can also be stored in the high house and low house without interfering with the loading of the throwing machines. The trap field house also has plenty of room to store an extra supply of targets. And some fields, both trap and skeet, are constructed so that instead of having a protection fence separating the fields, the barrier is in effect a long target-storage shed about four to six feet wide.

THE TARGET-SETTING HOOP IN SKEET

The target-throwing machines are usually set before the day's shooting takes place, preferably under a "no wind" condition. Once set, it should not be

Clay targets are purchased by the case, with 135 targets to the case. A case weighs thirty pounds.

necessary to change the spring tension during the shoot, unless the spring becomes defective. In skeet, the machine's spring is adjusted to a tension that will just reach the sixty-yard stake, passing near dead center in the *target-setting hoop*. The hoop, a three-foot circle of steel rod or copper tubing (which is lighter and will not rust) is held in position alongside the center stake or target-crossing point, 13½ feet above the ground. The post to which the hoop is attached may be of wood or, better yet, of a straight length of copper tubing (to which a copper hoop can be soldered). The ideal arrangement is to have a two-inch pipe set in the ground, as the target crossing point stake, and stuffed with sand or other material up to ground level. Then the post can be set into the pipe when the hoop is being used.

With the hoop having a three-foot diameter and the post being 13½ feet high, the center of the hoop will be located at fifteen feet, establishing the official target-height at that point. If both high house and low house targets whiz through any part of the hoop and land in the vicinity of sixty yards from the trap house the field is considered to be legal. The target-setting hoop is a piece of permanent equipment at all skeet fields.

Leonard Nicholson and coed Grosvie Robinson, members of the Yale Skeet Club, check target flight in the morning's calm air. The center of the 3 foot diameter hoop is 15 feet from the ground. The low-house targets emerge from the machine at three-and-one-half feet above the ground. The high-house targets fly out at a height of ten feet above the level of the shooting stations.

THE TARGET-MEASUREMENT ROD IN TRAP

The official ATA rules for target flight in American trap specify that "targets, whether single or doubles, shall be thrown between eight and twelve feet high, ten yards from the trap. The recommended height is nine feet. The height at a point ten yards from the trap is to be understood to mean height above an imaginary horizontal straight line drawn through the firing point and the trap."

Generally, if trapshooting targets fall between forty-eight and fifty-two yards in a straight line from the trap house (fifty yards is the recommended distance) they are legal targets and the height is usually considered acceptable. To meet the requirements, an appropriate measuring rod should be devised, one that will take account of the drop in terrain below that of the shooting stations.

173

A length of any type of pipe, about an inch in diameter, will do as a measuring rod. While being held vertically ten yards straight ahead of the trap in a line with Station 3, the pipe should be wrapped with a piece of tape at a point level with the grade of the station. Then the targets should fly between eight and twelve feet above the tape marker. The eight and twelve foot points on the pipe should also be marked with tape.

If the grounds have more than one trapshooting facility and the terrain in front of the houses is not at the same level, each trap field must have its own target-measuring rod, if the field is to meet official ATA rules concerning target flights.

18 - Reloading

WHAT IS RELOADING?

Reloading is a "do-it-yourself" process by which an empty shotgun shell is reconstructed to form a new shell that is as useable and as potent as the original. (Rifle and pistol cartridges can also be reloaded.)

When a shotgun shell has been fired, its components—pellets, wad, and powder—are discharged. The hull or shell, including brass head and detonated primer, remains in the gun until popped out of the chamber by the ejector. It is this empty hull that is retrieved before or after it hits the ground and saved for reloading.

WHY RELOAD?

The primary reason for reloading is economy. Generally speaking, a box of shells can be reloaded for almost half the cost of manufactured shells. For avid trap and skeet shooters, reloads can provide a substantial financial saving over a year's time. Actually, the advent of the plastic hull, and the development and availability of a wide selection of manual reloading machines, at least partly is responsible for the ever increasing number of participants in the clay target games, as well as for the upsurge of collegiate shotgunning. Without the financial advantages of reloading trap and skeet shells, the collegiate world of recreational and competitive shooting would soon fold.

GETTING STARTED

Getting started is easy. If the beginner does not have a friend to instruct him, easy-to-follow instructions can be found in the free pamphlets and brochures made available by such manufacturers as Winchester-Western, Remington, Dupont, and Federal. Also very precise step-by-step directions are presented in booklets that come with every new reloading machine. Many manufacturers produce the machines, which vary in price and capability.

RELOADING MACHINES

The type of reloader a gunner uses depends upon how often he shoots. A single gunner who shoots two to four boxes a week can get by with an inexpensive type of reloader, one that is capable of reloading perhaps one box of twenty-five shells in an hour's time. At the other extreme are the large reloading machines installed at some clubs for use by members. These can produce as many as 600 shells an hour.

The most popular reloaders lie in between these extremes. They produce between 100 and 250 rounds per hour. Any reputable gun and ammunition supply store can supply price information and the addresses of the manufacturers. The National Shooting Sports Foundation, as well as the manufacturers of the shell components, such as Winchester-Western, Remington, and Dupont will supply information if contacted by mail.

COMPONENTS

The components—shot, wad, powder, and primer—all come neatly packaged. The shot usually comes in twenty-five-pound canvas or cloth bags; the wads are carried in plastic containers, usually in lots of 250; powder is available in metal cans of various sizes; and the primers are housed in shallow trays, usually one-hundred to the tray. Fish and game clubs usually purchase components in large quantities for resale to members; their prices are usually lower than those of the clubs and gun shops. They are priced individually or by the lot.

THE OPERATION

Operating a reloader is so simple and the results are so gratifying that the beginner will be amazed. The sequence of steps is as follows: decapping the hull; seating the primer; dropping the powder charge; seating the wad; dropping the shot charge; crimp-starting; final crimping.

SAFETY

Two principal safety concerns must be exercised. The powder and primer must be properly stored, and the reloader must be alert while reloading.

Although care should be taken in all reloading activity, the activity is not unusually hazardous. According to figures taken from manufacturer's tabulations, about sixty percent of all ammunition reloaded in America consists

Storing reloading components safely.

of shotshells. That amounts to 600 million rounds annually! The great majority of these are loads for trap and skeet shooting. Misinformation about safety factors therefore should not deter the beginner from doing his own reloading.

The following paragraphs were taken from a booklet published by the National Shooting Sports Foundation:

STORING RELOADING COMPONENTS

Contrary to popular belief, modern *smokeless powders* do not create an explosion hazard. They don't even create a fire hazard if properly stored. In fact, smokeless powder is less flammable than many liquids commonly kept in the home, such as solvents, cleaning fluids, and polishes. Powders can be safely kept in the home by taking these steps:

Keep propellent powder in the container in which it was originally shipped or stored. These containers are specially designed to prevent explosion and spontaneous combustion. Never store powder in a severely confining container.

177

Powder containers should be kept under lock and key in a wooden cabinet. The heat-conducting properties of metal cabinets make them hazardous in the event of fire.

Propellent powders should be stored away from fire hazard areas. However, they should not be kept in either damp cellars or unventilated—and possibly very hot—attics, since they will ultimately deteriorate under such conditions.

Similar rules are applicable in storing primers. They should be kept in the original package until used and stored in a locked wooden box. In addition, the National Fire Prevention Association suggests limits on the number of primers that should be kept in the home or transported by vehicle: 10,000 in the home and 25,000 in any vehicle.

If reloading components are kept in the home in large quantity, it is a good idea to check fire insurance policies to make certain that coverage is not affected by the presence of primers and powders. Also look into state and local fire regulations to insure that storage and quantity limits are met.

Detailed information on the storage of reloading materials is available from the National Fire Prevention Association, 60 Batterymarch Street, Boston, Mass. 02110 (request NFPA Booklet No. 495).

The next two treatments are quoted from a booklet issued by Winchester-Western, titled "Ball Powder Loading Data For Shot Shells, Center Fire Rifle and Pistol Cartridges."

RELOADING PRECAUTIONS

Follow these precautions to help assure maximum enjoyment and safety in reloading and to assure uniform performance of your reloads. Remember that you can be badly injured or suffer severe burns if the strictest safety precautions and housekeeping rules are not enforced.

1. Exercise care at all times and wear safety glasses while reloading.

2. Never load in haste; avoid distractions.

3. Never smoke while handling powder or primers or during the reloading operation.

4. Handle primers carefully; they are the most hazardous of all components used for smokeless powder loads.

5. Keep powder and primers away from heat, sparks and open flames.

6. Store powder in a cool, dry place at all times.

7. Never use a powder unless you are certain of its identity.

8. Do not mix powders.

9. Devote full attention to reloading operations; avoid distractions.

10. Keep powder and primers out of reach of children.

11. Use components as recommended; don't take shortcuts.

12. Never exceed maximum recommended loads.

13. Develop a loading routine to guard against mistakes.

14. Examine every shell or cartridge before loading to insure good condition.

15. Double check every operation for safety and uniformity.

16. Check powder charge level in shells to avoid double charges.

17. On new center fire loads, start with charge weights ten percent below recommended maximum loads, except as noted in data.

18. Always watch for indications of excessive pressure.

19. Do not decap live primers; it is safer to destroy them by firing the empty cartridge or shell in a firearm.

20. Do not substitute components; it will result in a significant change in ballistics, and could result in an unsatisfactory or even dangerous load.

21. Do not allow children to play in the vicinity of handloading operations.

22. Observe all local fire regulations and codes with respect to quantities of powders and primers stored and conditions of storage.

23. Store powder only in its original container. Never transfer it from one storage container to another since this increases the possibility that it may become mislabeled.

24. Keep these "Reloading Precautions" posted where you do your reloading. Reread these precautions periodically.

RECOMMENDATIONS FOR STORAGE OF SMOKELESS POWDER

STORE IN A COOL, DRY PLACE. Be sure the storage area selected is free from any possible sources of excess heat and is isolated from open flame, furnaces, hot water heaters, etc. Do not store smokeless powder where it will be exposed to the sun's rays. Avoid storage in areas where mechanical or electrical equipment is in operation. Restrict from the storage areas heat or sparks which may result from improper, defective, or overloaded electrical circuits.

DO NOT STORE SMOKELESS POWDER IN THE SAME AREA WITH SOLVENTS, FLAMMABLE GASES OR HIGHLY COMBUSTIBLE MATERIALS.

STORE ONLY IN DEPARTMENT OF TRANSPORTATION APPROVED CONTAINERS. Do not transfer the powder from an approved container into one which is not approved.

DO NOT SMOKE IN AREAS WHERE POWDER IS STORED OR USED. Place appropriate "No Smoking" signs in these areas.

DO NOT SUBJECT THE STORAGE CABINETS TO CLOSE CONFINEMENT.

STORAGE CABINETS SHOULD BE CONSTRUCTED OF INSULATING MATERIALS AND WITH A WEAK WALL, SEAMS, OR JOINTS TO PROVIDE AN EASY MEANS OF SELF-VENTING.

DO NOT KEEP OLD OR SALVAGED POWDERS. Check old powders for deterioration regularly. Destroy deteriorated powders immediately.

OBEY ALL REGULATIONS REGARDING QUANTITY AND METHODS OF STORING. Do not store all your powders in one place. If you can, maintain separate storage locations. Many small containers are safer than one or more large containers.

KEEP YOUR STORAGE AND USE AREA CLEAN. Clean up spilled powder promptly. Make sure the surrounding area is free of trash or other readily combustible materials.

As mentioned previously, informative booklets concerning reloading tips, procedures and safety considerations are available from Winchester-Western, Remington, and the National Shooting Sports Foundaton. The National Reloading Manufacturers Association (NRMA) publishes a booklet that describes reloading in all its facets, and it is directed towards new shooters and new reloaders. The booklets are available, for a small fee, from NRMA, Suite 601, 1220 SW. Morrison St. Portland, Oregon 97205.

19 - Referees

Three types of referees officiate trap and skeet during competitions. First, and by far the most numerous, are the volunteer referees, who may or may not be completely familiar with all the technicalities. Generally, however, an experienced squad of shooters will police each other and will advise the referee, who may simply be doing the squad a favor by pulling and scoring. Obviously, the advantage of a volunteer referee is that he doesn't have to be paid, although he should certainly be thanked for his help. Such a referee serves adequately at week-end recreational shooting at the local club. But where serious competition takes place the referee, if he is a volunteer, must have had experience in competitive gunning. If an organization must rely on volunteer referees for its more serious intra-club tournaments, the volunteer should be from another club.

The primary reason why experienced volunteer referees are difficult to secure is because the job is a thankless one. Very few clubs show any real appreciation for this type of service. Refereeing in a competition requires standing for hours and being extremely alert; it is a long, tiring job. Most of the time the shoot management forgets about the volunteers. A show of appreciation, such as bringing him a drink and a doughnut or a sandwich, will go a long way towards persuading him to volunteer again. A gift box or two of shells with a "thank you" note attached will help immeasurably. Perhaps an arm band stamped REFEREE may appeal to the volunteer; it will give him some recognition. Shoot managers should not take the volunteer referee for granted.

The second type of referee is the experienced shooter who is paid for his services by being allowed to shoot for free. This type of refereeing, obviously, has severe drawbacks, for both the referee, who is to participate in the shoot, as well as for the other shooters in the competition.

Hiring a professional, full-time referee is, of course, the best arrangement. Such an official is expected to set the machines for target flight, distribute squad sheets, call the squads, and in general run the fields. Such an arrangement takes the load off the shoulders of the shoot management in controlling the fields. In large tournaments, management goes berserk trying to satisfy everyone; a paid professional referee, in most cases, is a God-send.

With some study and much practice, any experienced shooter can become an NSSA licensed referee. If you are interested, the procedure is simple.

First, join the NSSA. You will receive a copy of the Association's most recent "Official Rules and Regulations." Study that manual from cover to cover. To be licensed by the NSSA, a referre must pass written examinations, given by his state associations or NSSA affiliated clubs. Eye examinations are also required. Official NSSA referee cards and emblems are given to candidates who successfully meet the requirements. (The applicant must have officiated over a minimum of 2,500 registered targets during the previous year to be eligible to receive the official NSSA referee emblem.)

One paragraph in the eight pages concerning referees in the NSSA "Official Rules and Regulations" states: "The field referee is responsible for the conduct of the shooting on the field to which he has been assigned. He shall have jurisdiction on the field used by other shooters and spectators. He shall be completely familiar with the shoot program and with the NSSA rules. He must be constantly alert, impartial, and courteous though firm in the handling of shooters."

If you believe you can handle the above situation, pay your NSSA dues, study the book, apply for the NSSA REFEREES STANDARDIZED EXAMINATION. And good luck! An NSSA corps of licensed, professional referees is desperately needed.

20 - Facilities

A shooting facility consists of ten major areas:

1. *The 300-yard shotfall zone* may seem excessively large for a safety drop zone for trap and skeet pellets. Actually, at that distance, the shot comes down harmlessly like very light rain. However, even at that distance, there is still a possibility of a pellet hitting someone's eye and causing serious injury, so we stick to the 300 yards. Of course, that prescribed distance is needed only in the direction of the shooting, and for the area in which the shot actually drops.

2. *The walks* are constructed of concrete or asphalt. Obviously, such factors as costs and climatic conditions are to be considered when the material is chosen. Professional advice should be sought. Rod and gun clubs, schools, and other organizations with limited budgets can build an attractive trap or skeet field without specially built walks. The stations can be outlined by sunken 2×4's cut and nailed together to form a three-foot-square frame; the wooden frame is imbedded in the ground and the exposed upper edges painted white or yellow. Another option is to make the stations out of three-foot-square slabs of concrete, about two inches thick and imbedded in the dirt to ground level.

The trap and skeet field layouts must be built to meet exact specifications. The most easily accessible and complete skeet field layout diagrams are found in the centerfold pages of the "Rules and Regulations" booklet sent to all members of the NSSA. The best trapshooting field outlines are included in certain pamphlets distributed by the NRA, and the manufacturers listed at the end of this chapter.

3. *The houses* can be constructed of various materials, depending upon the financial condition of the organization building them. They can be made of wood, of cinder or concrete blocks with wooden stairs, or they can be built with a combination of wood and blocks. International skeet uses the same houses as American skeet. Also, the modified clay pigeon event is accommodated by the same house as that used in American trap. International or Olympic trap requires a highly technical and very expensive construction involving a pit housing fifteen target throwing machines. The NRA is the organization to query for detailed construction plans.

4. Each of the electrically controlled *skeet machines*, one in each house, throw targets in one set direction. The body of the machine does not move.

Flags add a fine touch of interest and color at the Yale University Fields.

The Club House.

184

Measurements for field layouts and height of trap machines must comply with official NSSA requirements. The style of the house, however, varies from one field to another. The protective structure separating the fields at the San Antonio facilities (top) also serves as a storage area for targets. The Yale University skeet houses and fences (center) are of a rustic design. Below: a typical trap house; more of it is underground than above ground.

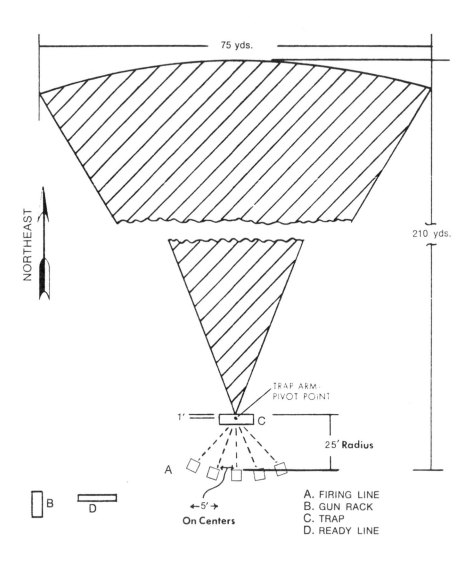

75 yds.

210 yds.

NORTHEAST

TRAP ARM·
PIVOT POINT

1'

C

25' Radius

A

B

D

←5'→

On Centers

A. FIRING LINE
B. GUN RACK
C. TRAP
D. READY LINE

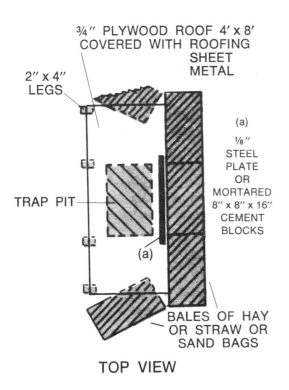

¾″ PLYWOOD ROOF 4′ x 8′ COVERED WITH ROOFING SHEET METAL

2″ x 4″ LEGS

(a)

⅛″ STEEL PLATE OR MORTARED 8″ x 8″ x 16″ CEMENT BLOCKS

TRAP PIT

(a)

BALES OF HAY OR STRAW OR SAND BAGS

TOP VIEW

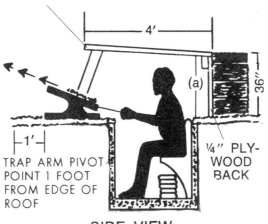

PLYWOOD ROOF COVERED WITH ROOFING SHEET METAL

— 4′ —

(a)

36″

—1′—

TRAP ARM PIVOT POINT 1 FOOT FROM EDGE OF ROOF

¼″ PLY-WOOD BACK

SIDE VIEW

The Mini-Trap is a qualification awards course involving a .410 shotgun that was introduced by the National Rifle Association. Mini-Trap uses standard clay targets, but the field is one-half the size of a regulation trap field.

187

Gun racks are necessary at the club house for shooters waiting for their squad to be called.

Trap and skeet facilities vary; some clubs contain a single field or two. Others are sophisticated establishments holding dozens of fields.

The target drops into position when the throwing arm is automatically cocked. The puller activates the mechanism by punching the appropriate button at the end of the portable cord.

The machines used for American skeet can be, and usually are, used also for international skeet. But the springs are wound tighter in order to throw faster targets. Also attached to the cord is a special electrical device that releases the target at an undetermined time—from the moment of the call until three seconds later, as prescribed by international skeet rules.

The *trapshooting machine*, on the other hand, oscillates back and forth. The gunner does not know in which direction the target is going to fly, because the machine's throwing arm is released in whatever direction it happens to be pointing when the release button is pushed.

The *modified clay pigeon machine* is different from the American trap mechanism in that it moves up and down, as well as oscillating back and forth, so that the height of the flying target is also unknown to the shooter.

Manual traps, far less expensive than automatic loading machines, require the manual loading of each target released.

Portable traps, the type that are used in informal shooting, such as in the novelty clay target games, are also part of the regular equipment at many trap and skeet fields. They are surprisingly rugged and light in weight. Some of them weigh no more than eleven pounds. They come complete and ready to use.

The "Trius Trap" (produced by Trius Products, Inc., Cleves, Ohio 45002), throws regulation targets, and does not require much effort to cock it. The trap is loaded by simply laying the bird on the arm, and the direction of target flight is ascertained by the position of the bird on the arm. Also the height of the target flight is determined by adjusting the trap vertically. By placing the clay target side by side on the arm, the trap will throw horizontal doubles. And when placing one bird on top of the other the trap will throw vertically spaced doubles.

Sporting goods stores that sell guns can help with information concerning portable traps.

A unique *portable trap unit* developed by the Missouri Department of Conservation has served well in the department's shotgun-instruction program. At a meeting of outdoor educators associated with a national convention, I discussed this portable unit with Bud Eyman who, among other duties, is the Hunter Safety Coordinator for the Missouri Conservation Department. Bud generously supplied the photos reproduced on pages 192–193 and the following information concerning the unit itself:

> The plank or board secured to the top of the house can be removed for transportation purposes. When the trap is in operation it is held in place by two wing nuts. The box or house is considerably narrower in width than the eight- or eight-and-a-half foot width or of the average trap house.

The Trius Trap Master is versatile. It pivots so that the operator can simulate regular trap targets or add variety or novelty to shooting. This machine throws targets of regular trap quality with horizontal and vertical variations. The Trius Trap Master does the job of throwing targets when the regular trap and skeet fields are occupied.

PORTABLE TRAP UNIT DEVELOPED BY THE MISSOURI DEPARTMENT OF CONSERVATION

A power winch is located between the two storage boxes and is used to load the trap house. The winch is plugged into the generator by use of an extension cord control.

Power is furnished by a government-surplus 110-watt generating unit. This gasoline power unit is transported a reasonable distance away to lessen noise at the shooting site.

The trap is a fully automatic Winchester trap anchored to the floor of the house which is constructed of full one-foot oak boards on full 4″×8″ oak skids. The plank secured to the top of the house is removable for transportation. It is 8′6″ long, the width of the average regulation trap house, thereby giving the shooter the exact width of a regulation house to sight on.

Setting up regulation distances from the trap house to the firing stations which are also portable.

Inside of skeet low house; showing hand-loading or manual trap.

The board or sighting plane, as it has been dubbed, actually serves two purposes. First, being eight-and-a-half feet long, it permits the instructor to refer to the standard five points of aim, as is common on a regulation trap field. Second, since the plank is painted five different colors separated by white lines, it serves as a teaching aid, since it establishes a point of reference to which that the student can easily relate.

The trap is a fully automatic Winchester trap anchored to the floor of the house, which is constructed of one-foot-wide oak boards on full 4″×8″ oak skids. Oak lumber was chosen because of its weight, which keeps the house stable during operation of the trap. Power is furnished by a government-surplus 110 watt generating unit. Once the trap has been removed from the trailer, the generator is transported a reasonable distance away to prevent the noise from the gasoline power unit from interfering with the instructors. A 200-foot electrical cable connects the two units. (The two boxes on either side of the generator are used to store clay birds

Western Autoloading Regulation Trap.

while transporting the unit. Each box will carry six cases of birds. See photo.) The trailer itself is a reconditioned boat trailer, with a steel bed replacing the rollers and skids used when hauling boats.

Unseen in any of the photos is a power winch, which is located between the two storage boxes and is used to load the trap house. The winch is plugged into the generator via an extension-cord control, for safety in case the cable breaks. The trap and house are winched up the conveyer tracks onto the trailer bed. (In the photo the winch cable has been drawn in.)

Western Autoloading Electric Trap (skeet shooting).

Since the unit was originally placed in service, we have found it necessary to make only minor alterations. However, we do plan to modify the trailer by making it tandem-wheeled for better weight distribution.

5. *Electrical systems*, of course, should be installed by licensed electricians. The specific plans and diagrams involved with electrical supply to target

196

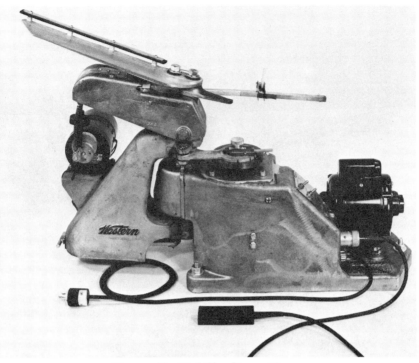

Western Modified Clay Pigeon Trap.

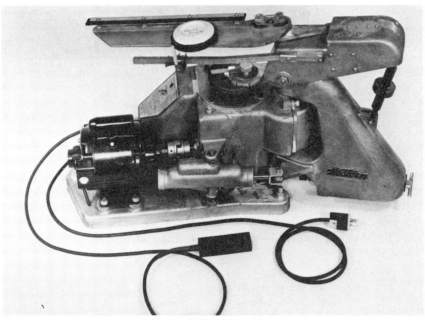

Western White Flyer Trap.

197

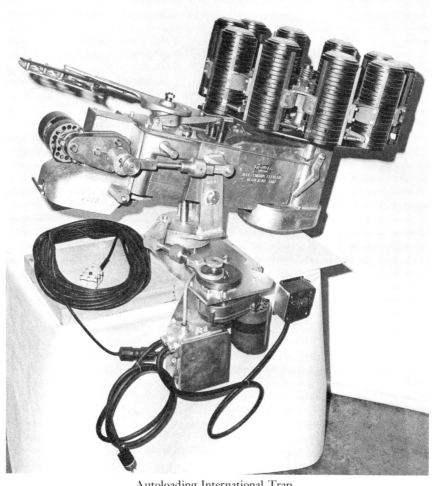

Autoloading International Trap.

throwing machines, and the machines themselves, are available from the companies that produce the traps, such as Winchester-Western. The layout for pole locations and estimates of the cost of erecting an electrical system may be obtained from the Muscatine Lighting Manufacturing Company, Muscatine, Iowa.

6. *Gun racks* are necessary at the shooting field, in shelters by the fields where gunners wait their turn to shoot, and also in the club house. At the field, the gun rack may be one of many designs, although they all basically serve the same purpose. The triangular type is the most popular. The racks

A gun rack at trap field.

Shelters close to the shooting fields are important to protect spectators and shooters from sun and rain. This one is at the Yale Outdoor Education Center Gun Club.

found in shelters are usually built in over one of the railings. And in the club house the racks are best recessed into a wall, so that people will not be tripping over a rack that has an extended base.

7. *Fences* are necessary to prevent spectators, as well as gunners who are waiting their turn to shoot, from encroaching too closely on the shooters. It is unsafe, and extremely disconcerting to the squad, if people are talking and moving about close to the shooting field. The fences can be constructed of attractive split rail or cedar, or they may have wooden posts supporting cattle fencing, or the fence may simply be composed of the least expensive posts available, erected eight or ten feet apart and connected by sections of rope. In other words, some sort of barrier should be erected, or a walkway established, as an indication that only shooters in action are permitted beyond it. There is a great laxity in many fields around the country, including some of the best, where persons not shooting jaywalk around the field because there are no visible restrictions.

8. At some fields, *shelters* may seem to be a luxury. But where no club house exists, or the club house is some distance away from the fields, a protective roof should be provided for squads of shooters who might oth-

erwise have to wait in the rain to shoot, or for interested spectators who might otherwise have to watch a particular shoot in the blazing sun. Shelters may be built in attractive and yet practical designs. The accompanying photos may be used as suggestions or guides that can be modified or embellished.

9. Shooting fields that are without club house facilities must provide (by law in most states) comfort stations: either outhouses or chemical toilets. The old time outhouse is not as unattractive as non-outdoorsmen may think. They require a minimum of maintenance. A five gallon can of powdered lime, with a scoop, should be provided. After each use, the pit should be lightly dusted with the lime, thereby keeping everything "sweet." Inexpensive lime available in hardware stores should be used.

Portable chemical johns can be rented for the season or for a particularly big tournament. The company that rents the johns also services them. On a year round basis, the portables, usually constructed out of durable but light plastic, should be purchased outright, and only the services contracted for. A sizeable amount of money can be saved that way.

10. The *parking area* should be placed as far as conveniently possible from the shooting fields. True, many people like to have their vehicle close by, not only as a convenience, but also because psychologically they can't bear to be out of sight of their car. Car parking should not be allowed close up against the fence of the shooting field. There is always noisy activity around cars, and that is a disadvantage to shooters.

Any person interested in constructing a trap or skeet field may obtain free, highly detailed plans, suitable for professional guidance, from the Shooting Promotions Departments of the following organizations:

Winchester-Western, New Haven, Connecticut 06515
Remington Arms Company, Bridgeport, Connecticut 06602
National Rifle Association, 1600 Rhode Island Avenue N.W., Washington, D.C. 20036.
National Shooting Sports Foundation, Inc., 1075 Post Road, Riverside, Connecticut 06878

APPENDIX

A - Instructor and Coach

Although the mechanics of instructing and the technique of coaching overlap in some instances, there is a notable difference between them. The instructor is a technician who grinds out the fundamentals of guns and gun safety, shells, targets, shooting procedures, field layouts, personal equipment, and costs. Beginners should be given a tour of the trap and skeet fields. They should view the inside of the houses and examine the trap machinery. In formal instruction, neophytes should be introduced to the history of clay target shooting and made aware of the benefits of this great outdoor sport as a healthy, life-time activity.

Ideally, newcomers should be introduced to all the fundamentals associated with guns and clay target shooting, but the instructor's most important function is to exercise a serious, no-nonsense approach to the thorough teaching of gun safety, gun handling, and gunology.

Although the roles of instructor and coach may be filled by the same person, the coach's duties are different from those of the teacher's. The coach is an analyst and an advisor. His primary responsibility is to observe the shooter, examine his shooting style and scoring performance, and then draw conclusions that will help the gunner's performance.

The coach's primary concern, obviously, is to improve the shooter's score. But he also has other responsibilities. He listens sympathetically to alibis and acts as both psychologist and disciplinarian. He arranges practice sessions, schedules shoots, and coordinates other team activities.

HOW TO PRESENT TRAP AND SKEET

New shooters should not be handed a gun and led onto the fields to shoot until they know what skeet and trap involves. Progressive instruction will be much easier if students are first made aware of the basics. First, a complete introduction to the physical aspects of the facilities is necessary. Whether instruction is intended for one person, a dozen, or a class of twenty or more, each novice should first observe a round of skeet and a round of trap. Two or three persons in an exhibition squad will do as well as a full squad of five; using a smaller squad will also save time. Next, each person should be shown the insides of the trap houses and the machinery while the instructor explains how the traps work and how the clay targets are loaded. For safety, the power should be shut-off and the trap arm released (not cocked) while the students are inside the house. During this introductory lesson the instructor need not take time to explain the composition of the clay target, its speed in flight, how many are packed in a case, etc. Such details should be reserved for the next lesson. At Station 1 or 7 on the skeet field, a few birds should be released, to show that the target's line of flight is always the same, although winds may cause slight variations. Targets should then be released at each station, as the referee does during a round of skeet. In this way, the students will realize that although the bird flight is constant, different kinds of shots are available at the different stations.

The instructor should plan this first lesson so that enough time is allocated to demonstrate the difference between the trapshooting set-up and the skeet. Back in the trap house, explain how the machine oscillates, causing the bird to fly out at an angle unknown to the shooter. Be sure to indicate how the machine can be set so that all targets fly out directly ahead, since that is the way the machine will be set during the first actual shooting lesson.

Important as it is to introduce new shooters to the physical aspects of the fields—houses, traps, and bird flight—it is equally important for the instructor not to dwell in any length on any portion of this introduction, because too much talking will simply turn the newcomers off. The potential shooter should be left looking forward to the next meeting.

The second part of the introduction to trap and skeet should take place indoors, if possible: in a school room, cafeteria, gymnasium, or club house, or wherever a blackboard and charts can be used effectively, and where the instructor does not have to compete with outdoor distractions. You will need a table on which to lay the guns and accessories. Incidentally, guns should always have their actions open and muzzle pointed away from the audience. Actually, disassembled guns are more effective for demonstrating lock, stock and barrel, and will also impress the group about safety concerns.

ORGANIZE A PLAN

Use the information found in other sections of this book to organize a lesson plan. Type the outline (all capital letters) and use double spaces between lines so that you can read it easily. Review it before the time of presentation. The depth and length of your presentation will depend upon the age and interests of the audience. The instructor may use the following skeleton outlines as models for his own plan.

The following outline is suggested as a guide for instructing a group of people whose main interest is in handling a gun and shooting either trap or skeet. In other words, the students need not be introduced to the many facets of trap and skeet that are not directly associated with actual shooting. You will want to adopt your own plan to suit weather conditions, time allotments, and other factors. The main ingredients of trap and skeet shooting, guns, shells, and targets, should be introduced to the group in that order.

1. Guns
Gunology and gun safety
Gun handling (carrying a gun, etc.)
Correct arm and leg positions

2. Shells
Diagram a shell on blackboard or use illustration
Explain components
Explain gauges and size of shot

3. Targets
Pass around a few clay targets
Explain composition of target and speed of flight
The necessity for wearing ear and eye protectors must also be explained. Then bring the group to the field. Take one person at a time to the shooting post. The remainder of the group should be sitting and observing within hearing distance.

OUTLINE II
This outline is more formal and complete. It is the kind the instructor should build on when teaching groups, clubs, or outdoor education and recreation classes that offer credit courses in clay target shooting.

1. Trap and Skeet Review
  a. History: how and why it all began
  b. Progressive steps of development, up to today's sophisticated matches and tournaments
  c. Statistics: number of shooters participating, geographical extent of clay-bird shooting (U.S., Canada, Europe). Female participation and accomplishments in trap and skeet
  d. Differences between: American trap, American skeet, International or Olympic trap, International skeet, Modified Clay Pigeon
  e. References: pamphlets, charts, books, etc.

f. Novelty clay target games: explain each game, use chalk drawing on blackboard, or illustrations

2. *Benefits to the Shooter*
   a. Lifetime sport
   b. No age restrictions
   c. Physiology and psychologically beneficial: relaxing, releases frustrations, outdoor sport
   d. Social aspects

3. *Cost Factor*
   a. How much will it cost?
   b. Load your own shells

4. *Personal Equipment*
   a. Ear and eye protection
   b. Shooting vests, belt pouch
   c. Clothing
   d. Footwear

5. *Guns, Shells, and Targets*
   As in Outline I, but in greater detail

EXAMINATIONS

Oral and written exams lend a tone of organization to the class, as well as keeping students alert. The instructor may also draw from any section in this book, provided, of course, that the questions used were covered in class.

GROUP OUTDOOR APPROACH

A definite plan of instruction should be followed when introducing trap and skeet to students or others who want to be informed about shotguns and the shotgun games, but do not necessarily care to become shooters. Usually, time is limited. Interest must be stimulated. Basics must be given. Each student should shoot a few times at the moving target. The Yale Forestry School, for instance, requires that its students have an introduction to shotgun shooting. Such a group is not interested in trap and skeet history, statistics, and other details of the sport. The students want to know what trap and skeet is, and want to be able to say they fired a gun. The instructor's lesson must be abbreviated but meaningful. It should emphasize gun safety

Teaching a group outdoors. The instructor must have a well organized plan of presenting safety concerns and basics of shooting. This troop of Boy Scouts is participating in the Annual National Hunting and Fishing Day activities at Yale University's Outdoor Education Center.

rules and should include a tour of the fields and the insides of a trap house. Above all, the instructor must work out a plan by which thirty or more shooters fire about three shots each. At the same time he has to keep the group from getting bored.

B - Methods of
Instruction

The best place to teach shooting is by the trap house at the trapshooting field. The gun, shells, and earmuffs can be conveniently placed on the roof of the house when necessary. The target throwing machine must be set to throw only straight-away birds. If the facility does not have a trap field, take the neophyte to Station 7 on the skeet field.

A portable trap can also be used for teaching, provided it is secured to a base or to the ground and throws targets consistently straight ahead. Use a hand trap only as a last resort, because the new shooter will be under enough stress without worrying where the target is going to fly. And use it only if you, the instructor, are capable of throwing straight-away targets consistently while standing to the rear of the shooter, (yet close enough to control his actions).

The autoloader is the appropriate firearm to use when teaching the use of a scattergun. The autoloader is easier to load and lock and has less recoil than other types of shotguns. The gun butt should be equipped with a recoil pad. The gauge of the gun to be used depends upon the age and physical structure of the learner. Most male teenagers, and some females, are strong enough to start with a 12 gauge. The majority of adult females however, and males twelve to fourteen years of age, usually should start with a 20-gauge gun. A single barrel 20-gauge "youth gun" works well for instructing young boys and girls. (See the section below on "Teaching Children.") Again, the instructor must use common sense. And he should remember to fit the gun and gauge to the shooter.

OUTLINE

Assuming that the new shooter has been given lessons in gun handling and gun safety, instructors will do well to follow the outline below in arranging an orderly and progressive plan for teaching shooting.

1. CHECK FOR DOMINANT EYE

If a right handed person's left eye is dominant he must shoot with that

210

eye closed. (A patch or a piece of tape placed over the left eyeglass lens makes this easier.) The alternative, shooting left handed, is rarely attempted. In any case, it is best to start the newcomer shooting with both eyes open. (See the section on "Sighting at a Target" in Chapter 11.)

Tom Prior, one of the finest of shotgun instructors, employs a hand trap and an equipment table to good advantage.

2. POSITION THE SHOOTER

Emphasize relaxed posture. The left foot should be forward (but not as far forward as in a rifle stance) and slightly bent at the knee. Elbows should be held as high as comfortably possible. The gun butt should be firmly set in the hollow or pocket of the shoulder.

3. CHECK FOR EYE ALIGNMENT ALONG BARREL

In order to bring the eyes into alignment with the barrel, the gun stock must be raised to the cheek. The beginner's usual tendency is to lower his head to the stock.

211

4. CHECK FOR PROPER SEATING OF GUN BUTT

One of the best methods of introducing the newcomer to correct gun positioning is to start by placing the gun on top of the shooter's shoulder, vertically, pointing the barrel to the sky. With left hand by his side and right hand holding the gun grip, the shooter then places his cheek on the stock and sights along the upright barrel. (See illustration.) Raising his left hand to grasp the forearm of the gun, and without changing angle of his head or arms he then lowers the gun to shooting position. As a result, gun butt will be placed where it should be: high, but completely in, and against, the hollow of the shoulder. The eyes will then be correctly aligned with the gun barrel and directed toward the target.

5. TAKE A REST

The instructor must realize that a person inexperienced with gunning will suffer from arm fatigue, not to mention the drain of energy caused by anxiety and apprehension, much sooner than practiced shooters do.

6. LOAD THE GUN

During the first lesson, the instructor should load the gun, giving the new shooter one less thing to worry about. While the beginner holds the gun with barrel pointed downward, the instructor slips the shell into the chamber and closes the breech.

7. FIVE SHOT INTERVALS

The average beginner should not fire more than five shots without taking a rest. If there are two or more pupils involved they should rotate, each firing five shells.

8. SWING AND FOLLOW-THROUGH

When a shooter becomes fairly proficient at hitting the straight ahead targets (hitting perhaps fifty percent of them), he should be taken about fifteen feet to the left of the trap house and given instructions on leg stance, gun swing, and follow-through. He should be told to point the gun ten to fifteen feet ahead of the house at shoulder height, and as the target flies out he should swing with it and fire the moment he feels the gun is slightly ahead of the target. The next five shots should be taken at an increased distance of about twenty-five feet from the left side of the trap house. Continue the same two exercises at the right side of the house. When the instructor is convinced that the shooter can load and handle the gun safely, and swing, lead, and follow through, he is ready for the trap or skeet field.

9. AT THE TRAP FIELD

If the potential gunner is interested in trap shooting, the machine's arm

212

The autoloader is the appropriate firearm to use when teaching a person to shoot a scattergun. It is easier to load and lock, as well as having less concentrated recoil than other types of shotguns.

is positioned to retain straight ahead throwing, but the shooter moves from left to right and fires at one or two targets from each of five spots about four or five feet apart. Then he moves back about ten feet and repeats the drill. His progress will determine when the machine should be readjusted to oscillate in regular trap routine. How many lessons or shots are required before the beginner is introduced to his first round of trap will depend upon the individual and the ability of his instructor.

10. AT THE SKEET FIELD

Station 7 is the place to start a beginner at the skeet field. The low-house target will not be difficult for the beginner to hit after the instruction he has received at the trap shooting field. The high house or incoming target is excellent for teaching the newcomer to lead the target, because plenty of time is available for eyeing the target and following it with the gun.

11. PROGRESS OF INSTRUCTION

Instruction should progress at a rate commensurate with the shooter's ability. After the beginner has become familiar with Station 7, take him to Station 1, where the incoming target is just like the one at Station 7. This

Yale coach Ed Migdalski with assistant coach Tom Migdalski instruct coed Marianne Gaertner, a member of the Yale Skeet Team. The coach should look for the basics: cheek away from stock, gun sliding from shoulder pocket, no follow-through, improper sighting along barrel, focusing on barrel rather than on target, foot and arm positions.

is an excellent place for the neophyte to practice following and swinging ahead, because the gun can be on target for practically the whole length of the field. Station 4 should be next in line because a long lead is required, which will impress the gunner with the fact that leads are different at each station. Instruction then continues at Stations 2, 6, and 8.

12. WORDS OF CAUTION
    a. Make sure the student wears ear muffs and eye protectors.

b. Check frequently to see that the gun is in the shoulder pocket; this will prevent muscle bruises.

c. Prevent fatigue. Space the shooting and do not rush the teaching.

d. Do not attempt doubles until the beginner has shot a few complete rounds.

e. Praise a hit. Discount the student's misses as unimportant.

f. The instructor should be at the beginner's side at each station until the shooter is completely capable of safe gun handling, and is thoroughly acquainted with the rules and regulations of skeet shooting.

TEACHING CHILDREN

The same principles that pertain to teaching teenagers and older persons to shoot, apply to instructing youngsters as well: patient progress in gradual and well-planned steps. The difference is that lighter guns and closer targets are used and work sessions are shorter.

The methodology of teaching shooting has been covered. However, the process of teaching children to shoot involves several basic factors that must be considered and applied intelligently.

Nancy and Tom Migdalski (age 4 and 6). Any youngster properly exposed to the shotgun games will benefit for a lifetime. Today, both are avid target shooters.

215

A boy can start learning to shoot at age ten to twelve, depending upon his physical development. Jim Dee, director of Winchester-Western's "father and son" programs, instructs young Tom Migdalski. Duncan Barnes and Bob Goss assist.

First, there is the question of age. When is the proper time to start learning to shoot? A husky boy of ten can handle a single shot 20-gauge "youth gun." Generally, about the earliest a child should begin taking lessons is between the ages of ten and twelve.

I exposed my son Tom to shooting at the age of six by bringing him out with me to the skeet fields. He didn't realize that he was being introduced to the clay bird sports. I made no attempt at showing him how the people were shooting. If he wanted to watch, okay; if not, okay. We wouldn't stay too long. But I was always sure that he had a bottle of pop and a doughnut at the club house (against his mother's wishes). In other words this experience was a fun outing and he began pestering me days in advance to "go to the club." That was good!

After several trips to the club grounds, I brought a .22 rifle and placed it on the rifle shooting bench, because Tom was too small to hold it. I let him snap off a few .22 shorts, just to let him hear the "bang." It wasn't many weeks later that he was shooting tin cans and enjoying it greatly. Young children have no interest in target shooting, but they love to see tin cans topple off a perch.

216

Two years later, when he was eight (which may be too young for some boys), I presented him with a single shot 20-gauge shotgun. His first lessons were nothing more than shooting at the bottom end of a five-gallon can (with permission of the club's management). From then on it was a matter of holding him down. Perhaps I started him too well, because today his main interests in life are trap and skeet shooting and duck hunting. In all the above I have tried to indicate that with children the teaching process must be gradual, above all it must be fun. Boredom will kill interest.

Other points to note: never try to teach beyond the child's attention span, which generally runs about twenty to twenty-five minutes. Start the youngster shooting a 20-gauge, single-shot gun. You will have to load the gun, and cock the hammer after he has put it to his shoulders. Be sure that the gun butt is equipped with a recoil pad, and that it is firmly bedded in the hollow of the shoulder. There is nothing that will discourage a young shooter as much as a bruised shoulder. Constantly check to see that the elbows are held high, which will keep the butt in place.

Encourage and praise the youngster at every opportunity.

Watch for signs of fatigue. All of the activity, besides the actual shooting, can quickly tire a young boy or girl.

During the beginning of a child's shooting program, do not dwell for any length of time on safety rules. You should never leave his side during the preliminaries. There will be plenty of opportunity to teach rules of safety and conduct when you start the child shooting clay targets. (The teacher should read the sections of this book pertaining to teaching and coaching and apply those principles when appropriate.)

AGE TO QUIT

Lessons in shooting can begin at almost any age. But when is it time to quit? One of the wonderful features of trap and skeet shooting is that one can enjoy the sport throughout one's life. Many national championships have been won by persons in their sixties and seventies. My friend Henry Alcus was seventy-seven when he tied his own veterans world record in the .410 event by shooting ninety-eight out of a hundred targets. That was a couple years ago and he is still going strong on the shooting fields!

Trap and skeet are such wonderful sports because everyone can enjoy them: young-sters, teenagers, middle-aged, senior citizens, and the handicapped. Mr. William Jacobsen of Omaha, Nebraska, who is 81, continues to shoot regularly.

C - How to Coach

"Behind it!" "Above it!" "Below it!" If that is your approach to coaching you are going about it the wrong way. Every shooter who reaches the point of hitting about fifteen out of twenty-five targets becomes an instant coach and uses that technique to advise other shooters. I have watched veteran shooters coach the same way. Such a method of coaching is a negative one and does nothing to improve the shooter's skill.

Instead of trying to diagnose where the shot pattern was in relation to the target, the coach should stand back and analyze the shooter. He should observe the gunner, not the target the gunner is trying to hit. If the shot pattern was behind the target there is a reason for it. To inform the shooter that his shot was behind the target is meaningless. But to tell him why he shot behind the bird is the intelligent and positive way of coaching, and it brings results. For example, the coach may notice the shooter stopping his gun swing. Rather than yelling "behind it," the wise coach should patiently explain the reason for the miss. "You stopped your gun swing, letting the target fly past the spot where you were pointing the gun when you pulled the trigger. Now, on the next bird, concentrate on staying ahead of the target and continue to follow through as you pull the trigger. It doesn't matter right now whether or not you hit the target. I want to see that follow through!"

TIPS TO COACHES

The most important subject that the coach must emphasize to his group is gun safety. And one of the most dramatic ways of doing this is to place a plastic jug, filled with water dyed red, on the ground. The jug could be set before the group arrives to the spot. Then, from a short distance away, the coach shoots directly at the jug. It bursts in an ugly way. The coach then picks up the remains and displays them to the group. The burst jug provides a graphic illustration of what could happen to somebody's guts if a shooter gets careless. The point should be reiterated: "Never point a gun in another person's direction!"

Another significant point that a coach must impress on his group is the fact that there is only *one* coach. Everyone on the squad will want to give advice to the person who missed a target. And it is the same old "You were behind it," or "You were above it." Sometimes three or four reasons come out of the same squad. This tends to be especially true if the shooter who missed the bird is a beginner.

COACHING NEW SHOOTERS

If the neophyte finds it unusually difficult to hit a target after being instructed in all the preliminaries, including a check for the dominant eye, the coach must do some analyzing. Of first concern is eyesight. Does the learner normally wear glasses but leave them off when shooting? How long ago did he have an eye examination? If no problem exists with eyesight the coach should focus his attentions, one at a time, on the five most common reasons why new shooters miss targets.

1. SIGHTING ALONG THE BARREL

All new shooters aim along the gun barrel while trying to fix it on the flying target. It is a natural thing to do. Although it is the most common fault of newcomers, and an extremely important factor in shotgunning, it is surprising how few coaches diagnose this problem. The usual instruction is "Don't aim, point the gun." Of course, that is good advice to someone who knows the difference between aiming and pointing. Most beginners however, will nod their head as if they understand, but they don't. The better approach is to say, "After you shoulder the gun and align your eye along the barrel, concentrate on the target, focus on *it* and not on the gun!"

2. PULLING CHEEK AWAY FROM STOCK

Another natural tendency for neophytes is to pull the cheek from the stock. Either the gunner is anxious to see whether or not he has hit the target, or he follows the bird with his eyes and leaves the gun behind. This fault is easy to diagnose by simply watching the shooter's head.

3. NOT FOLLOWING THROUGH

If the shooter is not following through, it is easy to detect because he is stopping his gun immediately after pulling the trigger. The fact that the target has flown past the spot where the shell pattern was pointed, because the gun was stopped, must be explained to the gunner on station. Emphasis on complete swing and follow-through will eventually eliminate the problem. Some shooters automatically stop their swing when the target is hit and the coach must make the shooter realize that the follow-through must continue whether the bird is hit or missed.

220

4. GUN BUTT SLIDING FROM SHOULDER POCKET

Another common fault with beginners is the sliding gun butt. If the butt is not properly secured in the hollow of the shoulder, two things will happen: the gunner will bend his neck downward so that his cheek will remain on the stock, and the recoiling gun butt will begin hurting the shoulder muscles. Most shooters will not admit that it hurts, but the next day's black and blue mark will be prominently displayed on the shoulder. Coaches should be on the alert for this problem. Beginners who are at first enthusiastic about learning to shoot will quickly lose interest if they are being hurt. This is especially true of females; they simply will not come to the field a second time if their first experience resulted in a sore shoulder. An ache in the shoulder caused by bad seating of the gun butt will also cause flinching, squinting, and even totally closed eyes when the trigger is pulled.

5. FOOT POSITION

Although foot position is one of the first facts of trap and skeet shooting taught to beginners, it is one that has to be keenly watched by the coach because the natural tendency of the human body is to direct the feet towards the starting point, that is, towards the skeet house where the target emerges, rather than to where the target will be hit. The same principle applies to coaching trap shooters. It is not sufficient to instruct the shooter in correct foot stance; he must be told why his feet should be positioned that way: "to enhance swing and follow-through, and to be in a natural, comfortable position at the time when you are firing ahead of the target."

The observant coach will find that beginners will often posture their feet more towards the house than they should. Such a stance causes the shot to emerge far behind the target because the gun swing and follow-through are being restricted by the articulation of the muscles and bones of the human body.

COACHING ADVANCED GUNNERS

More often than not, coaching advanced gunners is more difficult than working with the raw product, the person who has never shot a scatter gun. First, the coach must be diplomatic, because the person who has been shooting over a period of years is likely to be sensitive to criticism, even if he seeks it and it is constructive. Second, the coach must be able to give a convincing reason *why*, for example, the shooter is missing at a particular skeet station, or *why* he is constantly missing an extreme right or left shot in trapshooting.

Among advanced shooters the most common impediments to expert shooting are: low elbows in holding up the gun and bracing it to the shoulder; excessive leaning forward; squatting (in various degrees of angulation); legs spread too far apart. If it seems to the coach that one or more of these glaring form deficiencies are causing the gunner to miss his targets, he should not inform the shooter in the presence of other shooters. A squatter, leaner, or leg spreader has acquired that stance because he believes it makes him appear to be a real "hot-dog shooter." If it seems that such a participant might, with help, become a benefit to the team, it is worth the coach's effort to correct the shooter's defective style. He should approach the shooter off the field and explain that improvement in his stance and posture will help his scores. The gunner should be assured that although his scores will dip until he gets used to the unaccustomed new shooting posture, his scores will ultimately go higher than they were originally. If his response to the coach's concern is luke-warm, or if he tries the suggested new system once to appease the coach, and then discards it, the coach will find his time better spent working with a coachable shooter.

Another method the coach can use to discover a shooter's weakness is to study the score pad of about 200 targets shot and note the particular station or stations that the shooter has missed regularly. Are the misses mostly at incoming or outgoing targets, or does this shooter have the most trouble with the birds that fly from the right or left? If, for example, the gunner is right handed and constantly hits the low-house targets, but misses more than he should from the high house, crossing from left to right, it invariably means that on the birds flying to the left, the right arm is pushing the stock into his face, but on the targets flying to the right his face leaves the stock.

If the score pad shows that the gunner's misses constantly occur at one or two stations, then the coach should spend some time alone with that shooter on those particular stations, having him fire until the fault is corrected. It is not uncommon for good shooters to suddenly start missing at a particular station or stations. And it is also common for such participants to slide into some elementary miscues: raising the head too high on the stock; pulling the face off the stock; flinching; pausing during the swing; starting with a light squat at a particular station and rising up as the target reaches the trigger-pulling point; or placing the feet incorrectly at a certain station (a symptom easy to miss if the gunner's stance is correct at the other stations). If the shooter's score card shows that his misses are always towards the end of the round it may indicate that the fatigue factor is taking hold; in such cases the fatigue is most often in the shoulders and arms. Coaching, as applied to these and other symptoms is nothing more than observing, diagnosing, and correcting.

NON-COACHABLES

In trap and skeet shooting, as in every other sport, non-coachables are a problem. A non-coachable may be a shooter who has tried to make a team but failed, because he refused to take the coach's advice. Or he may have made the team but remains a mediocre shooter because he insists that he knows more than the coach. Or he may be the kind of person who is unable to receive instruction from anyone on any subject. Such an attitude will not change, and there are probably many more such prima-donnas in trap and skeet shooting than there are in such sports as football, basketball, or baseball. Shooters having the ability and experience to shoot in the area of twenty out of twenty-five targets need special handling. Those that will take coaching will be a blessing to the coach. Those who openly resent criticism should receive no further attention. The experienced coach should recognize such a situation as unchangeable and save himself much frustration.

POINTS FOR THE EXPERTS TO CONSIDER

When expert shooters of equal ability meet in an important competition, the final standing invariably shows that only a few missed targets separate them on the score board. After such a tournament, the best of shooters will ponder over particular targets missed: "Did I flinch at that station?" "Was my concentration interrupted?" "Was it a slow pull?" The few targets missed by the accomplished tournament competitors may not have been caused by one of the common faults discussed above. The difference between a shooter being in contention and falling out of the final championship competition may be the result of factors never considered by the gunners. Let us review some of these points:

When was the last time you had your eyes examined? As one grows older, eyes change and periodic exams are necessary. A slight change in eyesight, without a compensating change in lenses, will affect your shooting.

Have you considered the fatigue factor? Young or old, if your arms and shoulders have had no exercise to keep them in condition, your shooting will unquestionably suffer. Do you do any walking? Regardless of the type of job you hold, walking is an important conditioner for trap and skeet shooting. If you haven't walked all week, walking and standing at the shooting fields will certainly enhance the fatigue factor.

Do you drink coffee before or in between rounds of skeet? Coffee is a stimulant that may rev up your nervous system to the point where it does more harm than good.

Are you aware that breathing cigar or cigarette smoke raises your blood pressure, whether or not you are the one doing the smoking? And that such a condition may subtly affect your shooting accuracy? Smoke inhalation is especially detrimental during cold weather when small club houses with no ventilation are packed with shooters trying to stay warm until it is their time to shoot.

Did you add a bit of fatigue to your eyes without realizing it by watching someone else's targets from the sidelines for too long a time before your squad was scheduled to shoot?

While on a station did you drop a shell and pick it up, or did you bend over to tie your shoe? Bending over and quickly straightening up to shoot may have affected your equilibrium, causing you to miss that particular bird that you recently hit without trouble. Also, as you grow older your eyes will not quickly adjust to focusing from near to far objects.

The above factors may be subtle and undoubtedly appear to be insignificant to most shooters. But I can assure you, from years of observation, that they are valid, and may make a crucial difference in the consistant accuracy of your shooting. Further treatment of the various aspects of this subject will be found in the chapters dealing with kinesiology, physiology, and psychology.

D - Trap and Skeet in Education

There is an important place for the clay target sports of trap and skeet in both the high school and the collegiate world. That fact is emphatically substantiated by the tremendous growth of intercollegiate shotgun shooting throughout the nation. The faculty and administrators of most of our universities now are leaning more toward the development of the life-time sports and de-emphasizing the highly competitive, so-called varsity sports. Consequently, trap and skeet activities find a special niche in the ever-increasing recreation and club sports programs.

Club sports programs provide an activity of some kind for every individual, regardless of height, weight, and physical prowess. And the activity of trap and skeet shooting are perfect examples of sports in which persons of small size and a no more than average degree of physical dexterity can excel. On the skeet field no one raises an eyebrow when a five-foot-four, 120-pound coed is outshooting a six-foot-two, 230-pound football player, and when the other members of the squad, shooting in the same score range, may include a "fatty" and a "skinny."

What is so special about the collegiate shotgun shooting activities? And what does it have that most of the other sports do not have? To my way of thinking they are especially valuable because they offer both recreation and competition, a competition that is friendly even if it is serious and tough. Both factors are apparent on a large scale at the National Intercollegiate Trap and Skeet Championships, held annually since 1969, where hundreds of students, male and female, representing about fifty colleges and universities from throughout the United States meet for several days of shooting. When in action, the teams work as intently and with as much dedication as any other athletic team. But when each squad finishes its course of shooting there is no animosity; instead, there are congratulations—or condolences—and always comraderie and much sociability.

What benefits does the individual accrue? No one can deny that competitive sports have a positive value in development of person and personality. I have seen remarkable changes of personality in some students once they have learned to shoot and compete; confidence has replaced shyness. All

Collegiate Montage

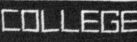

students want to excel, although the desire may be hidden at times. Trap and skeet offers them an opportunity to be good at something. Shotgunning, by its very nature, demands self control, concentration and, most importantly, discipline. It also has tremendous value as a way of releasing tension. It can be immensely satisfying and healthy for a student to let go of pent-up classroom frustrations by getting outdoors and banging away at fast flying targets.

Trap and skeet are now accepted as unique educational tools and valuable recreational and competitive activities for students in high schools and colleges. They will continue to be accepted as such, unless undue importance begins to be placed on winning, rather than on the recreational aspects of the sport.

College students interested in forming a shotgun club should contact their school's Student Union or Club Sports Department. Full time students are eligible to participate for four years in formal collegiate clay target shooting programs, including the regional and national championships. Graduate students, as well as undergraduates, are eligible.

E - Organizations

The four most important organizations in the United States dealing with shotgunners and the clay target games are: the Amateur Trapshooting Association, the National Skeet Shooting Association, the National Rifle Association (Shotgun Division), and the National Shooting Sports Foundation, Inc. The International Shooting Union is the parent body that controls international competition.

AMATEUR TRAPSHOOTING ASSOCIATION

A regulatory body for competitive trapshooting, the Interstate Trapshooting Association, was formed in 1892. Eight or ten years later this organization began promoting National Championship shoots. It was from these beginnings that the Amateur Trapshooting Association (ATA) was founded in 1923 in Vandalia, Ohio. A year later the permanent home grounds were built there.

The Association is the focal point of all registered trapshooting in the United States and Canada, and it computes and records the results of all registered trapshoots in the two countries.

Annually, each member of the Association receives a card on which are recorded his averages and handicap for every registered target shot in the preceding year. Also recorded are the member's scores and percentage average of hits on each of his handicap and doubles targets. The gunner's handicap yardage is punched along the edge of the card at the time of mailing. These cards must be presented to the management of any registered shoot in which the member wishes to participate. By using the data on the card, the shoot supervisor assigns the proper yardage and classification to each gunner.

Every registered trapshooter in the United States, Canada, and several foreign countries is listed by State, and in alphabetical order, in the Association's "average book," which is available from the ATA office for a nominal fee. The shooting ability, that is, handicap yardage, etc., of over 50,000 shooters can be easily ascertained. All members also receive the official ATA monthly magazine TRAP AND FIELD.

Annually, the ATA supplies, minus cost to the State Associations, silver awards (belt buckles, ladies' compacts, silver service, etc.). These attractive and functional awards are presented to the winners of the various State tournaments.

The ATA sponsors the Grand American, the largest of all participating sport tournaments (see Chapter 2). This spectacular ten-day shoot has been conducted on the Association's home grounds in Vandalia, Ohio, since the field's completion in 1924 (previous tournaments having been held in different parts of the country).

Every gunner in the United States and Canada interested in trapshooting will want to join the ATA. The dues are minimal and an informative magazine is distributed to the membership monthly. Application blanks are available from the ATA office, Vandalia, Ohio, 45377.

NATIONAL SKEET SHOOTING ASSOCIATION

In a manner similar to the Amateur Trap Association, the National Skeet Shooting Association (NSSA) is the governing body for all official skeet shooting activities in the United States. In the NSSA book of "Rules and Regulations" the Association is described as a nonprofit organization owned and operated by and for its members: sportsmen who are dedicated to the development of those qualities of patriotism and good sportsmanship which are the basic ingredients of good citizenship, and in general to the promotion of the interests, welfare, and development of skeet shooting and related sports. (A brief history of the NSSA can be found in Chapter 1.)

In addition to governing the present American or regulation skeet most commonly shot in the U.S., the NSSA has an international division for gunners who wish to shoot under the rules used in international competition (using the low gun position and variable timing of target release). As the controlling center for all registered skeet shooting in the United States, the Association computes and records the results of all registered shooting. All members of the Association receive the monthly SKEET SHOOTING REVIEW. In the "Records Annual" of the REVIEW the yearly national averages of all NSSA members are published. Like ATA members, each NSSA member annually receives an averages and handicap card, on which is recorded every registered target he shot during the previous year. The gunner's handicap yardage is punched along the edge of the card at time of mailing. The card is shown to the manager of any registered shoot in which the member wishes to participate during the current year. The shoot manager, by using the information on the card, assigns the proper classification to each participant.

The Association hosts the prestigious NSSA Annual World Championships. This week-long event is described in Chapter 2.

In 1970 the NSSA inaugurated a Hall of Fame to honor its people who had contributed greatly to the development of the game or who had been outstanding competitors over a lengthy period. Six famous gunners were elected the first year, and five more have been added each year since. The names of the distinguished members of this famous institution are usually listed in the "Records Annual," which can be purchased from the NSSA.

The home grounds and headquarters of the NSSA are located at the beautiful grounds of the National Gun Club in San Antonio, Texas. Membership applications may be obtained from most gun clubs or by writing to NSSA Headquarters, P.O. Box 28188, San Antonio, Texas 78228.

NATIONAL RIFLE ASSOCIATION

Strange as it may seem to the uninformed, the National Rifle Association (NRA) is an important organization in relation to shotgun shooting and the clay target games. Its influence in developing and encouraging international competition in Modified Clay Pigeon and International Skeet is especially notable. The International Shotgun Department of the NRA has a close working association with the International Shooting Union and is the leading proponent of developing International Skeet and Modified Clay Pigeon in the United States. The NRA also contributes to other less exotic, but nonetheless important, phases of shotgunning intended for shooters of different ages and different abilities.

The Association's Shotgun Qualification programs, including International courses, with awards (medals, pins, brassards, certificates) for designations of Marksman, Sharpshooter, Expert, and Distinguished Expert are especially attractive. The NRA offers a special program of classification and awards in the game called Mini-Trap (discussed in Chapter 7). Zone championships, U.S. International Skeet and Clay Championships and many other shotgun programs are fostered by the NRA.

The Association's AMERICAN RIFLEMAN magazine, sent to all members, covers international and National skeet, trapshooting, shotguns, shells, reloading, etc. All sorts of booklets and pamphlets concerned with shotgun activities and information such as how to build facilities, organize clubs, etc. are also available from the NRA (shotgun division), 1600 Rhode Island Avenue N.W., Washington, D.C. 20036. The annual membership fee is minimal. Any shooter interested in any of the above should join the Association.

NATIONAL SHOOTING SPORTS FOUNDATION, INC.

The National Shooting Sports Foundation (NSSF) was chartered in 1961 to promote the shooting sports in America and to give the public a better understanding of recreational shooting. It continues to play an active role in educating the public in the safe use of sporting firearms and in furthering the conservation of our natural resources.

The Foundation's center of operations, located at 1075 Post Road, Riverside, Connecticut 06878, also supplies informative brochures and pamphlets dealing with shotgun sports, firearms ownership, etc.

The NSSF is supported by over 130 firms involved in all aspects of the shooting industry. It has led the movement to make the National Hunting and Fishing day an annual event.

INTERNATIONAL SHOOTING UNION

The International Shooting Union (ISU) with headquarters in Wiesbaden Webergrasse 7, West Germany, is the international sports governing body for shooting. Over one hundred shooting federations from approximately one hundred countries comprise the union. The ISU standardizes rules, course of fire, targets, firearms, ammunition and the sportsmanship of in-

232

ternational shooting matches. It also controls the conduct of shooting events at the Olympic Games, Pan American Games, and several regional or sectional games. The ISU also sponsors the World Shooting Championships every four years, midway between the Olympics, as well as frequent World Moving Target Championships.

A great many men of medicine participate in the clay target games—a good indication of the health benefits to be derived from trap and skeet shooting. Members of the International Health Sciences Institute have formed the International Medical Skeet Association. Founded in 1972 as a corporation in the state of Nebraska, IHSI membership is composed of doctors who enjoy and participate in registered skeet shooting. They have their own events at a number of large skeet shoots, including the NSSA World Championships. Membership in the IHSI is open to any NSSA members who are doctors.

Winchester-Western officials who participated in the opening ceremonies of the Oliver F. Winchester Shooting Fields at Yale University's Outdoor Education Center were, from left to right: Lloyd Pierce, Jim Dee, Arnold Rohlfing, Charles Hays, and William Talley. Ed Migdalski, director of the Center and its shooting facilities stands to the extreme right.

Yale University was the nation's leader in establishing trap shooting as a competitive Intercollegiate sport in the early 1900's. (From left to right): C.P. William '23, Playford Boyle '23, Robert Brown '22 Mgr., Richard Gale '22 Capt., James G. Bennett '22, and Samuel H. Blackmer '24.

F - The Fundamentals of Clay Target Shooting

IF YOU WOULD SHOOT WELL . . . YOU MUST FIRST LEARN TO SHOOT PROPERLY

What are the basics? If you can see the target—with either normal eyesight or corrected vision—and have average coordination, you can learn to hit moving targets with a shotgun. All that's needed is a little concentration on the idea that you can . . . and will . . . hit the target.

The important things to learn in shooting at moving targets are:

A. PROPER STANCE
B. CORRECT GUN MOUNTING
C. THE RIGHT SIGHT ALIGNMENT
D. THE NEED TO LEAD THE TARGET
E. THE IMPORTANCE OF SWING AND FOLLOW-THROUGH

Let's take them in step-by-step order, beginning with:

A. PROPER STANCE

Your body must be under control at all times, not tense but alert and expectant. A comfortable stance that permits good balance at the instant you wish to hit the target is of prime importance. To achieve this:

1. In skeet shooting, face the approximate spot in the target's flight path where you expect to shoot at the target. This will normally mean in the vicinity of Station 8, near the center of the skeet field. Turn half right and space feet comfortably apart.
   In trap shooting, the positioning of your feet will vary from station to station. The proper stance for each one will be covered in the trap section further on.
2. Shift body weight to ball of left foot, but do not permit the left hip to move forward. Rather, lean the shoulders and trunk of body slightly forward. Bend left knee just a bit.
3. The right shoulder is raised and pushed forward into the shotgun's buttstock.

4. The cheek is laid firmly against the side of the gun stock.

B. CORRECT GUN MOUNTING

See page 139.

C. THE RIGHT SIGHT ALIGNMENT

A shotgun must be mounted properly in order to hit flying targets consistently. When the gun is brought up in correct position to your shoulder, face, and eye, it will shoot exactly where you are looking. Properly mounting the shotgun also accomplishes a second function: it provides the right sight alignment. With practice you should be able to mount your gun and merely look at the spot where you choose to have the shot charge go when you pull the trigger. To do this:

1. Grip the gun firmly, the left hand extended under the fore-end and the right hand grasping the pistol grip—thumb around grip, not alongside.
2. Keep the head erect and raise the gun toward eye level so that the front sight appears to rest on the top of the gun's receiver (the metal part just forward of the pistol grip). With your right shoulder raised, and jutted slightly to the front, the buttstock can now be pulled firmly into proper position on the shoulder.
3. Make sure the butt rests on the shoulder, not on the upper muscle of the arm.
4. Your right cheek should be nudging the side of the gun's stock, or comb as it is commonly known. Now that your gun is properly mounted, you will automatically have correct sight alignment. You can forget the sights and concentrate on the target.

D. THE NEED TO LEAD THE TARGET

Lead, or forward allowance, is the compensation that must be made in order to hit a moving target. Imagine trying to direct the stream of water from a garden hose at a youngster running across your lawn. If he were some distance from you, and traveling fast, you would have to swing the hoze nozzle ahead of him, and keep it swinging, in order to douse him.

Though a clay target moves a lot faster than a youngster, and a shot charge outraces a stream of water, the basic principle is very similar. Since, in skeet, or trap, the targets are ejected at a constant speed, the amount of lead changes only in relation to the angle of the target to the shooter. These angles change as the shooter moves around the field from station to station.

E. THE IMPORTANCE OF SWING AND FOLLOW-THROUGH

Simply moving the gun to a point ahead of the target and stopping as you fire is not enough. Think back to the garden hose. As you swung the nozzle out ahead of the running youngster, you had to continue swinging—maintaining your lead—at a constant speed to keep the stream of water hitting him. So, too, must the shotgun be kept swinging as, and after, the trigger is pulled. Imagine that the garden hose, instead of shooting a steady stream, were equipped with a trigger that released but a short burst of water. Now you have a rough idea of how the shot charge behaves on its way to the target.

COORDINATION OF MIND AND BODY

In shooting, as in most worthwhile endeavors, achievement of perfect co-ordination of mind and body is the result of continued practice. To the new shooter, the smooth, fast, precision displayed by the expert may seem be-yond normal ability. It is not. Through application of the fundamental prin-ciples, development of proper form and consistency of technique, the expert has established a pattern of well conditioned mental and physical reflexes only by practice. It goes without saying that your first few times out on the shooting field will find you somewhat lacking in the full coordination you will attain later on. Don't worry about it, simply resolve to improve with more frequent practice.

Having familiarized yourself with the fundamental guideposts—proper stance, correct gun mounting, the right sight alignment, need to lead the target, importance of swing and follow-through, and coordination of mind and body—you are ready to put the basics to work. To do this, let's try a round of skeet first and then move on to the trap field.

FOR A STARTER: *Let's try the high house target shooting from Station 4.*

On Station 4 you will notice that you are standing mid-way between the high house on the left, and the low house on the right, in the middle of the semi-circle's perimeter. Your target will come from the high house, on your left. Now, ready yourself to break that target:

1. Assume the proper stance—remember, this means facing the approxi-mate spot in the target's flight path where you expect to shoot at the bird. In this case, slightly to the left of the Station 8 position at the center of the field. Turn half right and space your feet comfortably apart, shifting body weight to the ball of the left foot. Bend that left knee just a bit and lean the shoulders and trunk of the body gently forward.

2. Mount your gun, left hand extended under fore-end, right grasping pistol grip—don't forget to place the thumb *around* the grip. Keeping your head erect, raise the gun toward eye level, so the front sight just floats on the top of the receiver. Raise and push your right shoulder forward as you pull the gun butt firmly into proper position—on the *shoulder*, not on the upper arm muscle. Nudge that stock with your right cheek.

3. Now, without moving your feet, turn your body toward the high house from which the target will come. Point the gun at a spot about three feet ahead of and just below the target-opening, on a line with the flight path the claybird will take.

4. Get set. When you call "Pull," the target will be released. The moment you see the target appear, start your swing, swiveling from the ankles up. As you catch the target, start swinging ahead of it to establish a lead of about four feet (the length of your gun). Maintain that lead, pull the trigger—but do not stop your swing—and follow-through. That puff of black dust out there means you paid attention, did everything correctly—and really powdered the target.

These photos illustrate the basic gun points and foot positions of correct trap shooting at each of the five stations. Note that the leg shadows accentuate the direction of foot placement. As shooters become experienced they may slightly modify gun points, leg postures and foot positions to meet their own physical characteristics. The new shooter should start with the positions indicated in the photo.

station 2

station 3

station 4

station 5

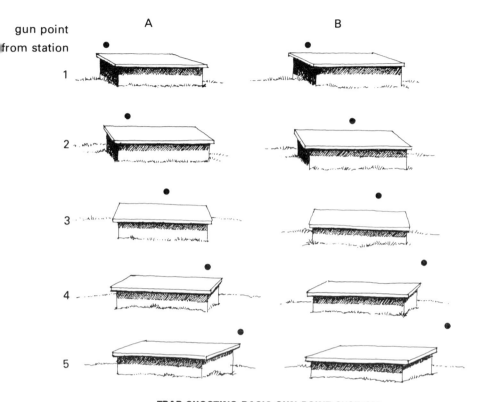

gun point
from station

A   B

1

2

3

4

5

TRAP SHOOTING BASIC GUN POINT SYSTEMS

In sixteen-yard trapshooting the above diagrams indicate the two basic gunpoint systems most commonly used by experts. Veteran shooters do not agree on which method is superior. The new shooter should try both methods and find which one best suits his or her personal physical characteristics. Slight modifications in gun point and foot position may also help at "trouble stations." A. Take gunpoint about one foot above front edge at all stations. (1) One foot inward. (2) Quarter of the way in. (3) Above center. (4) Quarter of the way in from right. (5) One foot in from right, or directly over corner. B. Take gunpoint (1) about 1½ feet high between middle and left front corner. (2) About 1½ feet high over middle of house. (3) About 2½ feet high, halfway between middle and right front corner. (4) About 2½ feet high over right front corner. (5) About 2½ feet high and 1½ feet to right.

Foot positions and gun points, Stations 1 through 5.

STATION 1

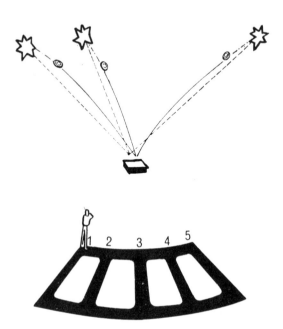

At Station One, your feet should be placed as indicated with the left foot pointed toward the left corner of the trap house. Your gun should point about one foot above and one foot in from the left front corner of the house. This point is shown here by a red dot.

Here, and in the next four diagrams, solid black lines indicate the flight angles of three typical targets you may encounter; dotted black lines indicate the swing and follow-through of your gun as well as the target breaking point.

SOME TRAPSHOOTING HINTS

Since there can be no practical rule of proper lead in trap, the new shooter must rely on adapting the basic principles he has learned about shooting at moving targets. The principles of lead, swing, and follow-through are applicable to all forms of shotgun shooting. In trap, just as in skeet, a stopped

242

STATION 2

STATION 2

At Station Two, your feet should be placed as indicated with the left foot pointed one quarter of the way in from left corner of the trap house. Your gun should point one foot above and about a quarter of the way in from the left front corner of the trap house, as shown by the black dot.

gun at the instant of firing is certain to cause a miss. Good stance and proper gun mounting are equally essential to the trapshooter.

Most trap targets are rising as well as going away from the shooter. Therefore, they require an upward lead in addition to whatever quartering lead

STATION 3

At Station Three, your feet should be placed with the left foot pointed slightly to the left of the center of the trap house as indicated. Point your gun one foot above the center of the trap house as shown by the black dot.

may be indicated. Remember to establish proper horizontal and vertical lead and continue your swing and follow-through as you fire.

As the new shooter gains experience through practice, he will gradually acquire a conditioned memory image, or mental picture, of how far over,

STATION 4

STATION 4

At Station Four, your feet should be placed as indicated with left foot pointed one quarter of the way in from the right corner of the trap house. Point your gun one foot above and a quarter of the way in from the right front corner of the trap house as shown by the black dot.

right or left to lead every target thrown. It will take time, but eventually each memory image—neatly tucked away and classified in the mind—will come flashing through with computer-speed to match every target angle encountered. Trite but true, practice makes perfect.

STATION 5

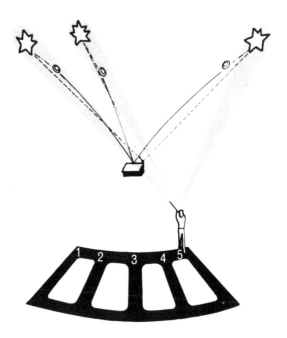

STATION 5

At Station Five, your feet should be placed as shown with the left foot pointed toward the right corner of the trap house. Point your gun one foot above and one foot in from the right front corner of the trap house, as shown by the black dot.

Some Skeet Shooting Hints

The illustrations on the following pages will show what to do in order to break high and low house targets at skeet stations 1 through 8.

STATION 1 HIGH HOUSE *Lead: 6" under*

STATION 2 HIGH HOUSE *Lead: 1'*

STATION 3 HIGH HOUSE *Lead: 3'*

STATION 4 HIGH HOUSE *Lead: 4'*

STATION 1 LOW HOUSE　　　　　　　　　　　　　　*Lead: 1'*

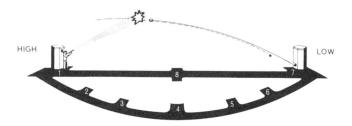

STATION 2 LOW HOUSE　　　　　　　　　　　　　*Lead: 2'*

STATION 3 LOW HOUSE　　　　　　　　　　　　*Lead: 3½'*

STATION 4 LOW HOUSE　　　　　　　　　　　　*Lead: 4'*

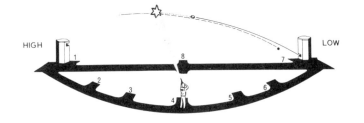

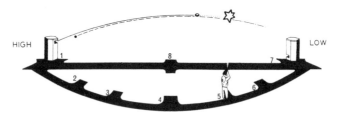

STATION 5 HIGH HOUSE *Lead: 3½'*

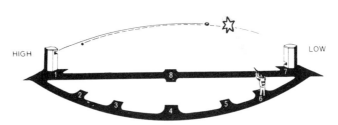

STATION 6 HIGH HOUSE *Lead: 2'*

STATION 7 HIGH HOUSE *Lead: 1'*

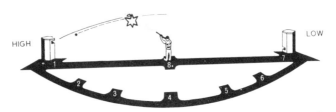

STATION 8 HIGH HOUSE *Lead: Blot out target with muzzle and slap trigger at same time*

250

STATION 5 LOW HOUSE   *Lead: 3'*

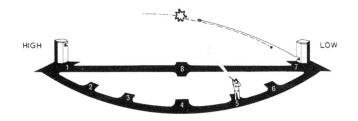

STATION 6 LOW HOUSE   *Lead: 1'*

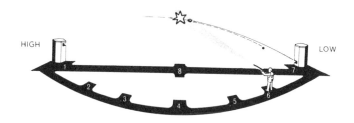

STATION 7 LOW HOUSE   *Lead: Point Blank*

STATION 8 LOW HOUSE   *Lead: Blot out target with muzzle and slap trigger at same time*

Index

255